The Liturgical Renewal
of the Church

ADDRESSES OF THE
LITURGICAL CONFERENCE

Held in Grace Church, Madison
May 19–21, 1958

BY

THEODORE OTTO WEDEL

MASSEY HAMILTON SHEPHERD, JR.

ARTHUR CARL PIEPKORN

ARTHUR CARL LICHTENBERGER

JOHN OLIVER PATTERSON

WILLIAM HAMILTON NES

Edited for The Associated Parishes, Inc.
BY MASSEY HAMILTON SHEPHERD, JR.

NEW YORK   OXFORD UNIVERSITY PRESS
1960

THE LITURGICAL RENEWAL
OF THE CHURCH

THE

Liturgical Renewal
of the Church

EDITED BY

Massey Hamilton Shepherd, Jr.

This book is the first attempt to give a comprehensive treatment of the thought and activity of the contemporary Liturgical Movement in the United States, inclusive of Protestantism as well as of Roman Catholicism. Though addressed primarily to Episcopalians, it is ecumenical rather than denominational in scope.

The addresses published in this volume, by five Episcopalians and one Lutheran, were first delivered at a Liturgical Conference held in Madison, Wisconsin, May 19-21, 1958, during the season of Ascensiontide. The conference was sponsored by Grace Episcopal Church in that city, as a notable part of the centennial celebration of the parish. Co-operating in this endeavor were the clergy and lay members of The Associated Parishes, a group intensely concerned with the liturgical revival in our times.

The following distinguished authors are represented: The Reverend Theodore Otto Wedel, Canon of

Washington Cathedral and Warden of the College of Preachers; The Reverend Massey Hamilton Shepherd, Jr., Professor of Liturgics, Church Divinity School of the Pacific; The Reverend Arthur Carl Piepkorn, Professor of Systematic Theology, Concordia Seminary; The Right Reverend Arthur Carl Lichtenberger, Presiding Bishop of the Protestant Episcopal Church; The Reverend John Oliver Patterson, Rector and Headmaster of Kent School; and The Reverend William Hamilton Nes, Professor of Homiletics, Seabury-Western Theological Seminary.

THE REVEREND MASSEY HAMILTON SHEPHERD, JR., who is Professor of Liturgics at the Church Divinity School of the Pacific, is also Director of the Graduate School of Theology of the University of the South and a Member of the Standing Liturgical Commission of the Protestant Episcopal Church Commission on Ways of Worship, World Council of Churches. He is the author of a number of books, including *The Living Liturgy* and *The Oxford American Prayer Book Commentary*.

liturgical movement - addresses, essays, lectures

In memoriam

JOHN HENRY KEENE

1904–1958

FOREWORD

THE addresses published in this volume were first delivered at a Liturgical Conference held in Madison, Wisconsin, May 19–21, 1958, during the season of Ascensiontide. The conference was sponsored by Grace Episcopal Church in that city, as a notable part of the centennial celebration of the parish. Co-operating in this endeavor were the clergy and lay members of the Associated Parishes, a group intensely concerned with the liturgical revival in our times. Since the inception of this group a little over a decade ago, the parish of Grace Church has been one of its strongest supporters both materially and spiritually. The episcopal patron of the Madison conference was the Right Reverend Donald H. V. Hallock, D.D., Bishop of Milwaukee, who, with his customary graciousness and interest, presided at several of the sessions.

It is indicative of the widespread concern for the subject

of the conference that, in addition to the many parishioners of Grace Church who attended, more than 130 persons, both clerical and lay, came to Madison at their own initiative and expense, and that too from all parts of the country. Though the conference was in the main an expression of concern for liturgical renewal on the part of members of the Episcopal Church, it will be readily seen from the papers here published that the topics were not considered from a merely denominational perspective. In particular, several of the addresses devoted much attention to the current Liturgical Movement in the Roman Catholic Church; and the presence and contribution of Dr. Piepkorn of the Lutheran Church, Missouri Synod, provided an ecumenical dimension to the discussion of liturgical revival in contemporary Protestantism. The comprehensive scope of the Christian gospel was effectively set forth in Dr. Nes's sermon, preached at the impressive Solemn Eucharist that concluded the conference.

In large measure, the success of the gathering at Madison was due to the devoted and skillful direction of the Rector of Grace Church, the Reverend John Henry Keene, D.D., who was also a charter member of the Associated Parishes. Dr. Keene died suddenly on August 19th, just three months after the conference. The great loss thus sustained to the liturgical leadership of the Church has brought to his many friends and admirers, at the same time, a more profound gratitude to our heavenly Father for the manifold gifts of grace exemplified in his life and ministry. To his memory this volume is fittingly dedicated. His colleagues in the Associated Parishes have established a 'John Henry Keene Memorial Fund,' in the hope of promoting other conferences and lectures on the liturgical life of the Church comparable to the one initiated at Madison under Dr. Keene's foresight and guidance.

MASSEY H. SHEPHERD, JR.
Editor, The Associated Parishes, Inc.

October 1959

CONTENTS

Page

I. THE THEOLOGY OF THE LITURGICAL
RENEWAL   3

The Reverend Theodore Otto Wedel, *Canon of
Washington Cathedral; Warden of the
College of Preachers*

II. THE HISTORY OF THE LITURGICAL
RENEWAL   21

The Reverend Massey Hamilton Shepherd, Jr.,
*Professor of Liturgics, Church Divinity
School of the Pacific, Berkeley, California*

III. THE PROTESTANT WORSHIP REVIVAL
AND THE LUTHERAN LITURGICAL
MOVEMENT   55

The Reverend Arthur Carl Piepkorn, *Professor of
Systematic Theology, Concordia Seminary,
St. Louis, Missouri*

IV. THE SOCIAL IMPLICATIONS OF THE
LITURGICAL RENEWAL   101

The Right Reverend Arthur Carl Lichtenberger,
*Presiding Bishop of the Protestant Episcopal
Church; Sometime Bishop of Missouri*

V. THE PASTORAL IMPLICATIONS OF THE
LITURGICAL RENEWAL   123

The Reverend John Oliver Patterson, *Rector and
Headmaster of Kent School, Kent,
Connecticut*

VI. THE WORD FOR ASCENSIONTIDE   149

The Reverend William Hamilton Nes, *Professor
of Homiletics, Seabury-Western Theological
Seminary, Evanston, Illinois*

INDEX   159

I

THE THEOLOGY OF THE LITURGICAL RENEWAL

The Reverend Theodore Otto Wedel,
Ph.D., S.T.D., D.D.

*Canon of Washington Cathedral,
Warden of the College of Preachers*

THE THEOLOGY OF THE LITURGICAL RENEWAL

THERE is one area of experience in which any one of us can speak with some authority: our own autobiographical story. Inasmuch as I am handicapped on loftier planes of authority, I venture to avail myself of this privilege—the story of my own adventures as amateur scholar in the area of liturgical theology. It lays claim to no final conclusions or encyclopedic learning. It may merely resemble a travelogue of a tourist visiting a strange continent for the first time. But such a visitor might see things which the local residents do not see because they take them for granted, and he might become a guide for other travelers similarly undertaking a first voyage of discovery.

The beginning dates back forty years. By way of a fortunate circumstance, I became acquainted during a residence in Minnesota with a remarkable Roman Catholic family. George Michel, a brother of a bridesmaid at my wedding, had recently become a Benedictine monk, taking the name in his Order of Father Virgil. Those familiar with the history of the Liturgical Movement will recognize the name at once as that of the virtual founder of the liturgical revival in this country—its home, the Benedictine monastery at Collegeville, Minnesota.[1] I had myself scarcely heard of the Liturgical Movement before my acquaintance with Father Virgil. But he had apostolic zeal in its behalf even in those earlier years

[1] A biography of Dom Michel has recently been published by Paul Marx, O.S.B., *Virgil Michel and the Liturgical Movement* (The Liturgical Press, 1957).

of his all-too-brief career. I listened to his rhetoric of enthusiasm with increasing appreciation, and became an amateur
liturgist in embryo. I fear I wearied Father Virgil, on occasion, by trying to convince him that Rome was merely, at a
belated stage, catching up with the Book of Common Prayer.
His Benedictine courtesy, however, was equal to such
dialogue encounters.

Interest in the liturgical revival, when once aroused, rarely
subsides entirely. I began to read the literature of the Movement in spare hours. Residence in a Minnesota academic
community gave place, in due time, to one in New York,
headquarters for my post as Secretary of College Work in
our Episcopal Church. I began to mention the Liturgical
Movement in talks to university audiences, but realized very
well that ignorance far outweighed intimate acquaintance.
By chance I heard that there was resident in New Haven an
expert in liturgical learning—the late William Palmer Ladd,
Dean of the Berkeley Divinity School. I made bold to ask for
an interview. This was graciously granted, and gradually I
presumed upon the kindness of the good Dean for a whole
series of dialogue sessions. By way of bibliographical advice,
Dean Ladd persuaded me that no deposit of liturgical learning was equal to the *Jahrbuch für Liturgiewissenschaft*, a
yearly volume of essays and reviews published by the Benedictines of Maria Laach, Germany. Despite budget difficul-
ties, I managed to secure most of the volumes published to
that date, and I began to read, still as an amateur, but under
Dean Ladd's guidance.

Hundreds of pages remained unread, but I did soon come
upon two major essays by Dom Odo Casel, in Volumes VI
and VIII, presenting what has come to be known in the
Liturgical Movement as *Mysterientheologie*, 'Mystery Theology.' The reading of these essays constituted a major, even

revolutionary, event in my imaginative understanding of the Eucharist. Whatever the critical evaluation of Dom Casel's theology may eventually turn out to be, I feel certain that his insights will not be ignored. His use of the word 'mystery' in place of the word 'sacrament' is in itself significant. The Latin term 'sacrament' was narrowed down, in medieval times, to signify a sacred thing. The older Greek term *mysterion* had a much wider meaning. It meant, first of all, an action, a re-presentation of an event, a recalling of the past so as to make it real in the present. Many of us are familiar with the Greek word *anamnesis*, signifying this remembering or recalling in the Eucharist of the whole series of events from the passion to the ascension of Christ. We have an echo of this ancient *mysterion* vocabulary in the phrase of our Prayer Book Consecration Prayer: 'the memorial thy Son hath commanded us to make.' According to Dom Casel, it is precisely this action-memorial of the sacrifice of Christ which *is* the offering or sacrifice of the Mass. The offering *is* the *anamnesis* itself. A past event becomes really present now. The very nature of a sacrament is this real presence of a past event in ongoing time.[2]

All this may not sound very revolutionary at first glance. But let any one who is not bound by scholastic philosophical dogmas play with the possible implications of this 'mystery theology,' and it yields startling results—too startling, perhaps. Note the use of the phrase 'real presence.' Mountains of controversy have belabored that concept. Heirs that we are of the medieval shift of meaning given to the word 'sacrament' from action to *thing*, we wrestle with the problem of how a spatial substance can be the vehicle of a personal

[2] 'We are acting Christ's death sacramentally'; Dom Anscar Vonier, O.S.B., *A Key to the Doctrine of the Eucharist* (Burns, Oates and Washbourne Ltd., 1925), p. 111.

presence. Some kind of space miracle is apparently involved. In the older, pre-medieval understanding of a *mysterion* or sacrament, so Dom Casel and his followers argue, the Eucharistic real presence miracle (to use that phrase naïvely for the moment) is first of all a time-miracle, not a space-miracle. The liturgical re-presentation or 'making memorial' of the sacrifice of Christ involves the employment of physical symbols, of course—water in Baptism, bread and wine in the Eucharist—and these play a necessary part in the action. Dom Casel pays repeated respects to the dogma of transubstantiation. But one representative of 'mystery theology,' after listing a roster of the ancient Fathers of the pre-medieval Church, summarizes their Eucharistic doctrine as follows: They all describe the Eucharist as the making present in time of the once-for-all sacrificial *act* of Christ. They ascribe to the humanity of Christ not only a new *ubicatio,* but to the past completed act of Christ a new *quandocatio'*—a time universalization in contrast to a space localization.[3]

Can the recovery of this pre-medieval understanding of the real presence in the Eucharist, as real presence in an action rather than real presence in a substance—or at least primarily the former—help to bridge the gulf in Eucharistic theology that has existed for four hundred years between Protestant and Catholic doctrines? At least one trusted Protestant theologian holds this hopeful view. Rudolf Otto, in an essay entitled 'The Lord's Supper as a Numinous Fact,' cites one of Dom Casel's definitions of the Mass as follows: The Mass—'a symbolic *act* which is imbued with the presence of the redemptive *act* . . . The Church through the solemn words of commemoration (the anamnesis) makes the *sacrifice* of Christ and thereby the redemptive *work* which culminated

---

[3] *Jahrbuch für Liturgiewissenschaft* VI (1926), 195.

in his death to be *present.*' Rudolf Otto then comments: 'If I understand these words aright, that is exactly the sense of my own exposition. We have to do then not with a transubstantiation of a physical *substance* into a hyperphysical *substance,* but with the transubstantiation of an event (namely the breaking of bread) into another *event* (namely the event of Golgotha).' 'Informing and underlying the celebration of this meal, the redeeming and atoning sacrifice on the cross is present, a new covenant between Deity and mankind, and in it, judging and saving, sensibly near, the covenant-making, mysterious God. This is, indeed, a Real Presence; what other presence is like this?'[4]

To those who have long grown accustomed, in their Eucharistic devotions, to center their reverence upon the elements on the altar, such a transvaluation of the concept of the real presence may come as a shock. Nor, as I shall venture to indicate later, is this the last word to be said on the subject. For the moment, I can only testify that a gradual, imaginative appropriation of this 'mystery theology' has meant for me a profound liberation from bondage to an apparently commanded devotional piety for which I was not mystically endowed. Moreover, this imaginative appropriation received buttressing and underpinning by two further insights which I encountered in my wanderings in the land of liturgical theology. I continue, accordingly, with my modest travelogue.

The first of these fresh insights was a new understanding of the genius of the Church's liturgical worship as a whole. Let me refer to the Church Year as an example. The observance of the festivals and seasons of the Church Year is clearly a consecration not of a substance but of time. It is, to employ a bold formula, a sacrament of time. Past historical

---

[4] *Religious Essays* (Oxford University Press, 1937), p. 52.

events become present in our experience here and now. Augustine, in a letter to Bishop Boniface,[5] calls attention to the fact that the Christian folk say or sing on a Sunday, above all in Eastertide, 'The Lord is risen today!' The use of the little word *is* symbolizes a time-mystery, a *mysterion*. How can a happening two thousand years ago become such an *is* today? And yet, it does. Baptism offers another clear example of this mystery. The substance-symbol of water used in Baptism cannot be given a meaning exactly parallel with that accorded to the elements employed in the Eucharist, though it seems clear that the early Fathers of the Church did not differentiate as between the symbols employed in the two major sacraments as sharply as did later liturgical understanding. We still, as a matter of fact, pronounce a kind of *epiclesis* ('invocation') over the water in the font. Be this as it may, Baptism is clearly a sacrament or mystery, making real a past event in present time. We *die* with Christ and are raised with Him *now*.

The second of these insights crossed my horizon of understanding of liturgical theology by way of the revived Biblical theology of our generation. Biblical scholars are clarifying for us the peculiar genius of the Hebrew mind and of Hebraic thought-forms. As these are contrasted with the nature-worship of the heathen religions of pre-Christian days and again with the religions regnant in the Hellenic world to which Christianity addressed itself, one such contrast emerges clear and firm. The concept of holiness in the Biblical view attaches itself to symbols of time; the concept of holiness in the Greek world (to limit the argument to the Christian era) attaches itself to symbols of space. Greek art, for example, is plastic, space-dominating, space-forming. Hellenic worship took

[5] *Epistles* 98, 9.

place in the presence of a statue of a deity—a 'graven image' in the eye of the Jew. To this spatial mentality of the Hellenic world, the mentality of the Hebraic world offers a striking contrast. The world of space is, of course, not ignored. This would have meant a disparagement of the works of creation. Even in the worship life of early Israel, the ark was a revered symbol, as was the Paschal lamb, and, of course, the Temple, though it is worth noting that the final disappearance of the ark from history caused the later Biblical writers apparently no concern. Despite the fact that time and space are inter-related in Israel's cultic development, space is not in control. In the Genesis account of creation, 'God blessed the seventh *day* and made it *holy*.' 'There is no reference in the record,' so a Biblical scholar comments, 'to any object of space that would be endowed with the quality of holiness. . . . Holiness in time, the Sabbath, comes first.'[6]

It is, furthermore, a commonplace in Biblical theology today that we meet in the Bible revelation of God in the form of historical events: God's mighty acts. God is the God who acts and speaks. Israel received the revelation by way of the sense of hearing, not sight. 'What the eye was to the Greek, that the ear was to the man of Israel.' 'To the ancient Israelite neither nature nor history *is*, but both are events, happenings. The "thing" is always the "thing done"; space is produced by event.'[7]

We can assume, surely, that this Hebrew mentality con-tinued into the days of the New Testament, and must have been shared by our Lord—'space is produced by event.' Even the command voiced at the institution of the Lord's Supper

[6] A. J. Heschel, *The Sabbath* (Farrar, Straus, 1951), p. 9.

[7] Cited from a privately circulated essay, *The Biblical View of Time*, by James Muilenburg, Professor in Union Theological Seminary, New York City.

is a verb: *Do* this [an action] in remembrance of me. St. Paul
defines the meaning of the Eucharist as showing forth 'the
Lord's *death* [again an action, an event] till he come.'

It is therefore quite understandable that representatives
of the *Mysterientheologie* find this view of the Eucharist as
a time-sacrament lingering long in the Church in the age of
the Fathers. Proof of reticence with regard to admission of
space symbols into the worship life of the Church is written
large in the iconoclastic controversies of the seventh and
eighth centuries. Icons were, at the close of the bitter controversy, admitted into the sanctuary. But even a cursory
reader of the story must be impressed by the fact that such
admission was very carefully guarded. No statue of the
Virgin or of a saint, let alone of our Lord, is to be found to
this day in any Greek Orthodox Church. The icon must obey
the laws of symbolic, not realistic art. A Raphael madonna,
for example, is unthinkable in an Orthodox shrine. This
anchorage of the early Church's liturgical theology in the
priority of symbols of time—of speech and of hearing—over
spatial symbols carried over also into the reticence of the
Fathers in rationalizing the real presence in the Eucharistic
elements. Bishop Yngve Brilioth explains the hesitant and
still ambivalent realism of the Fathers in their dealing with
the doctrine of the real presence in the Eucharistic bread and
wine as evidence of 'the reluctance of theological thought to
tie down the heavenly Lord to the categories of space.'[8]
Indeed, if the liturgiologists of the school of Maria Laach
are right in returning us to the vivid time categories of early
liturgical thought, our own Anglican Fathers, inheritors as
they were of medieval misunderstandings, may have been
wiser than they knew, when they declared that 'Transubstan-

[8] *Eucharistic Faith and Practice, Evangelical and Catholic,* au-
thorized translation by A. G. Hebert (S.P.C.K., 1930), p. 61.

tiation (or the change of the substance of Bread and Wine) in the Supper of the Lord . . . overthroweth the nature of a Sacrament.'

Inasmuch as my discussion has taken the form of a personalized travelogue in the land of liturgical theology, I can report that appropriation of the full implications of a return to pre-medieval understanding of the Eucharist takes time, but also that it is very rewarding. The controversies, for example, that have surrounded the word 'sacrifice' in connection with the Eucharist are largely laid to rest. The Mass is obviously a sacrifice. Liturgical apprehension needs merely to rediscover the true nature of a sacrament as past event made present to relieve many of the scruples which have haunted Protestant conscience on this issue.

Nevertheless, I would not blame the student of *Mysterientheologie* if he confessed that the last word has not been said on the doctrine of the real presence in the Eucharist. We still confront the obvious fact that substance-symbols, symbols in the category of space, do play a necessary part in sacramental worship. Granted that the Biblical theologian quoted earlier is right in asserting that in Hebraic thought 'the "thing" is always the "thing done"; space is produced by event,' the thing is still there to be dealt with and must receive meaning. The words of institution recalled from the account of the Last Supper contain not only the words 'Do this in remembrance of me,' but 'This *is* my Body; this *is* my Blood.'

If we turn to the 'mystery theologians' for light on this issue of the real presence conveyed to us by way of a spatial symbol, as well as by symbols in the category of time, we discover that they, too, do not ignore the problem. As already noted, Dom Casel refers repeatedly to the official Roman dogma of transubstantiation and takes it, as it were, in his stride. He is aware of the fact that the Eucharist is not only a re-presentation of the sacrifice of Christ, but also a Holy Communion. Just how Roman Catholic liturgiologists would deal with the problem of according full weight to the verb *is* in 'This is my Body,' if they were freed from the tyranny of Aristotelian metaphysics, we do not know. But they do feel at liberty to say enough to help us who are not under that tyranny. A quite remarkable suggestion that a new way may be found to reconcile the apparently conflicting views of real presence in time and real presence in space is contained in a parenthesis, tucked away in a footnote in Dom Gregory Dix's *The Shape of the Liturgy*.[9] The footnote reviews the transubstantiation controversy—almost the only allusion in the 750 pages of his masterpiece to this difficult topic. 'I do not know,' says Gregory Dix, 'that any thoroughgoing attempt has ever been made to state the truth along the lines of a theology of the eucharistic action instead of in terms of the metaphysical correlation of the elements with the Body and Blood.' Yet this is precisely the clue which the pre-medieval understanding of the Eucharist as real presence of the dramatic action of Cross and Resurrection as an integral whole may contain. Accord priority to real presence in this Eucharistic *action*, and real presence in the symbols of the sacrificial victim naturally follows. But, to cite Dom Casel himself: 'Only the presence of the sacrifice as action gives meaning to the presence of the One sacrificed.' Or, to cite further: 'The secondary significance of the Eucharist, namely, its claim to be supernatural food, derives from its primary significance as an offering; for the Holy Communion is a partaking precisely of *sacrificial* food [*Opferspeise*], Body and Blood of a crucified Lord.'[10]

[9] (Dacre Press, 1945), p. 630.
[10] *Jahrbuch für Liturgiewissenschaft* VIII (1929), 195, 181.

There runs through the writings of the 'mystery theologians' a passionate concern that the Eucharist, paralleling all the sacraments in this regard, conveys to the worshipper not merely the presence of the Person of Christ, but the presence of His saving work. If the coming of the incarnate Lord into our human life had stopped short of the Cross and Resurrection, would there have been a gospel to proclaim? The Church's memorial sacrament cannot stop short with the Incarnation either, however real that presence might be made to reappear on the Church's altars. Some, at least, of the causes of the Reformation revolt against medieval Catholicism was insight into this simple fact. Vision of a holy thing, even if a transubstantiation miracle were accepted, is not yet a drinking of the cup of the new covenant. Real presence of the crucified and risen Lord must involve action as well as vision and sight.

My travelogue might end here. Yet the account would omit one large area of new understandings without which even this brief sketch would be incomplete. It has, indeed, an important bearing upon the doctrine of the real presence itself.

No reader of the literature of the liturgical revival can fail to note that it is beginning to confront the Church with the need for dealing seriously with the doctrine of the Holy Spirit. A recent theologian has called this doctrine the 'stepchild of theology.' The systematic theologian has been afraid of it. The Spirit 'bloweth where it listeth,' and the learned doctors of the schools, if they want to observe it so that they can devote to it at least one chapter in a textbook, must step out of the classroom and themselves 'go to church.' But, clearly, no theology of the sacraments dares to ignore it.

For example, the moment that we employ the phrase 'real presence,' we confront it, as it were, 'head-on.' Just how can

Christ risen, ascended, and sitting at the right hand of the Father, be present at or on thousands of altars on earth at the same time? The liturgical theologian will reply that He is present as the 'pneumatic' Christ, Christ as Holy Spirit. 'According to Apostolic language,' so Dom Anscar Vonier reminds us, 'it is Christ who hides after He accomplished His work on earth, and it is the Holy Spirit who is made manifest. The Spirit is the true theophany after Christ's ascension till the Lord returns again from heaven in the glory of the Father.'[11] Very well. The 'real presence' of Christ, then, must be the real presence of the Spirit; and the primary localization of the Spirit, if localization in space as well as time is looked for, is surely in the Church itself. Let us, accordingly, listen to Dom Anscar Vonier further:

The Eucharist is not a heavenly mystery; it is directly an ecclesiastical mystery. When the Church celebrates the eucharistic mysteries she does not stretch forth to the unseen regions of heaven; she is not laying hold on a distant Bridegroom; she sends forth no piercing cry to call Him down from the skies. On the contrary she enters into herself, she utters words of power, a power that resides within herself. . . . The Son of God places Himself in the very bosom of the Church in that great mystery, not through an independent deed of His, but through the sacramental act of the Church. He is not like a guest who comes and goes; He is more like a child whom the Church takes into her arms.[12]

But the Church is the Body of Christ thus present in its midst as Holy Spirit. The Church offers bread and wine on an altar; and in so doing, as St. Augustine has taught us, the

[11] *The Spirit and the Bride* (Burns, Oates and Washbourne Ltd., 1935), p. 14.
[12] Ibid. pp. 226-7.

Church offers itself. At the Holy Communion, the Church unifies itself by all members partaking of the one loaf and of the one covenant cup. Surely the real presence of the Spirit continues to abide in the fellowship of the Spirit throughout this action-drama; and even humble things of earth, bread and wine, become action-symbols in the mystery, vehicles and means utilized by the Spirit to create or re-create the unity of the Body of Christ. 'Whatsoever comes into contact with the Holy Spirit is hallowed and transformed,' so reads a sentence in the ancient liturgy of Sarapion. Spirit and body are inseparable in human experience.

Dare I venture upon a humble analogy? It is taken from our common corporate life. Every human grouping engenders, or is possessed by, a spirit, an *esprit de corps*. Every human grouping maintains its unity through sacramental means, the spirit of the group transforming visible symbols or actions into vehicles of corporate unity. Picture, for example, a birthday party in a home—a family circle celebrating a kind of secular Eucharist. The party would be unthinkable without the presentation, at the climax of the festivity, of a birthday cake. Every member of the family shares in an eating ritual. Aunt Sally, however, is ill and had to miss the birthday party. Cousin Susie reverently cuts a piece of the birthday cake, wraps it in a napkin, and carries it to the family's absent member. Aunt Sally, in turn, partakes and is sacramentally united with the family circle. Cousin Susie may never have heard of 'reservation,' but, on a secular plane, she has practised it nevertheless.

Can we fully rationalize what has happened? I doubt it very much. Yet we take such experiences in our stride in our common life. A spirit—the spirit of a united family circle—has somehow utilized as vehicle of spirit power and spirit presence a 'thing,' a mere product of the baker's art.

The Eucharist, in its turn, may remain forever a mystery unrationalized. But the Church down the ages has known from experience that in its sacrament of unity it meets its Lord. It unites itself with Him as present through His Advocate, the Holy Spirit. But the unification does not end there. The Church participates in His saving *work* as well—His passion, resurrection, and glorious ascension. The saving acts of Cross and Resurrection are made present as action-mystery here and now, not by way of sentimental recalling, but by 'the memorial' Christ has commanded us to *make*. We *do* this *anamnesis* in remembrance of Him.

Rudolf Otto, the Protestant theologian cited earlier, may be right when he adds to his words of appreciation of the mystery theology of Roman Catholic scholarship the comment that, on the strength of the recovery of this understanding of the Eucharist as first of all real presence in time, 'the separated denominations may yet find common ground in a part of their doctrine and practice which is now a painful source of estrangement between them.'[13] My own explorations in the land of liturgical theology, limited though they have been, have led me also to embrace this hopeful mood. Most of the new insights into the Church's worship life that I have met in my voyages of discovery come out of the writings of Roman Catholic pioneers. Are we witnesses of an ecumenical miracle? As Anglicans we are freed from many of the confessional tyrannies which still hamper our Romanist brethren from making full use of their prophetic insights. We are similarly freed from the confessional tyrannies that bind the Spirit's 'blowing where it listeth' in our sister communions of the Reformation exodus from papal rule. Ours is the Church of Common Prayer, called of God, as many among us at least

[13] Op. cit. p. 52.

see our vocation, to witness to this liturgical symbol of unifying power in our divided Christendom. But is it still fully *Common* Prayer among us? Is cultic chaos threatening our vocation? Is the Eucharist, the sacrament of unity, a cause of disunity among even ourselves, as it has been tragically such a cause in the past history of the people of God?

All of us surely are called—Romanists, Protestants, Anglicans all—to return to the rock whence we were hewn, the 'making memorial' in sacramental action of the Cross and Resurrection of our common Lord, His sacrifice made present *now*. Imbedded in the ancient Roman Eucharist itself is this utterly simple, yet ever inexhaustibly mysterious call to the whole people of God: '*Do* this in remembrance of me.' I can, in fact, find no better ending to this travelogue than to cite one of the majestic strains of the most ancient and primitive Roman Mass:

> Unde et memores, Domine, nos servi tui
> sed et plebs tua sancta
> eiusdem Christi filii tui domini nostri
> tam beatae passionis
> necnon et ab inferis resurrectionis
> sed et in coelis gloriosae ascensionis
> offerimus . . .

> Wherefore, O Lord, we thy servants, together
> with thy holy people,
> mindful of the blessed passion
> of the same Christ thy Son our Lord
> as also of his resurrection from hell
> and his glorious ascension into heaven,
> offer . . .

II

THE HISTORY OF THE LITURGICAL RENEWAL

The Reverend Massey Hamilton Shepherd, Jr.,
Ph.D., S.T.D., D.D.

Professor of Liturgics,
Church Divinity School of the Pacific

THE HISTORY OF THE LITURGICAL RENEWAL

The Roman Catholic Church

THERE is no individual who is competent to give a sufficient account of the liturgical renewal in our times. Contemporary movements always present peculiar obstacles to the chronicler of their history. The sources are too scattered and much of them inaccessible. Hence they cannot be properly collated and evaluated. If the movement is promoted by a sufficient organization, with a secretariat that keeps records, the task is, of course, much easier. Such is the case with the Ecumenical Movement. Despite its vast dimensions, the progress of Christian unity in the past fifty years can be chronicled with a fair degree of accurate perspective and proportion. One can point precisely to dates of appointment of specific commissions, conferences, negotiations, and to consequent achievements and failures.

The problem is different with the Liturgical Movement. Its scope is even more vast than the Ecumenical Movement, for it includes the great Roman Catholic communion. But the liturgical revival has no central organization responsible for its promotion. Its story differs in each of the several Christian bodies affected by it, for each one presents a peculiar complex of circumstances and problems, many of which can only be understood and properly evaluated by one who stands inside the corporate life of the particular communion concerned. The interaction of influences of liturgical renewal among the several Churches of Christendom occurs through an indefinable free play of ideas and personal acquaintances. It rarely involves an inter-church group participation.

Only in the Roman Catholic Church has the liturgical revival had a strong organizational leadership and, within quite recent years, the highest official support and direction. For this reason, the history of the Liturgical Movement can be more adequately recounted for the Roman Catholic, than for other Churches. For the same reason also, the ideals and practices of liturgical renewal in the Roman Catholic Church have exercised a predominant influence upon the thinking and programs of liturgical leaders in other Christian Churches. The Roman Catholics have produced the most extensive literature on the subject, in all languages and at all levels, from scholarly treatises to popular tracts. They have organized by far the largest number of liturgical conferences, both for clergy and laity, and have brought together in both national and international gatherings the ablest and most concerned leaders of the movement.

Yet because of its policy of nonco-operation with other Christian bodies, at least officially, the Roman Catholic Church has largely excluded from all its several activities in liturgical revival the active participation of members of other Churches who are deeply interested in the movement. There have, of course, been many friendly conversations and exchanges of a personal nature across the ecclesiastical barrier. And the Benedictine monasteries of the Roman Church, both in this country and abroad, have been most gracious and hospitable to visiting non-Roman Catholics who have sought to study their aims and ideals at close range within the corporate life of their communities. But the fact remains that

the impact of the liturgical revival in the Roman Catholic
Church upon other Christian Churches has been indirect and
undirected. Its progress and goals have of necessity to be
studied from the outside, so to speak, through the initiative
of individuals who are interested.

Another factor that has prevented a full appreciation of
the creative elements in the liturgical renewal of the Roman
Catholic Church, on the part of those who stand outside of
it, has been the large attention necessarily given by the
Roman Catholic leaders in the movement to problems
peculiar to the life of the Roman communion itself. I refer
to the extensive discussions concerning the use of the vernacular in the liturgy, to the complications of adjusting liturgical experiment to the intricate corpus of canon law, and
to the restrictions laid about theological speculation by the
rigid dogmatic structure of the Roman Church.

All this being said, it remains necessary nonetheless to
understand the successive phases of development of the
liturgical revival in the Roman Catholic Church, in order to
place this movement in all its varied aspects in Western
Christendom as a whole within a proper chronological perspective. For out of the history of this movement in the
Roman Church, one may construct a pattern of development
that may serve as a convenient frame of reference for studying its progress, in varying degrees of advancement, in other
Christian traditions. To date, the liturgical revival in the
Roman Church has exhibited three major phases or periods,
though one must always bear in mind that each of these
phases rests one upon the other, and that the peculiar interests of each period are carried over and extended into that
which follows it.

The first of these three periods may be described as the
recovery of the Church's true liturgical tradition. It is a time

when leaders are primarily concerned with the history and
authority of the Church's official liturgical rites as they have
been inherited from the past. The second phase of the movement opens when this work of historical restoration is trans-
mitted to clergy and lay leaders of the Church through an
organized program of education in the meaning of the liturgy
and its place in the total life of the Church. This second
phase moves inevitably into the third, the practical application of a true liturgical spirit and life among all the faithful—
what has been called the Pastoral-Liturgical Apostolate. Yet
it must be emphasized again that the work of the first two
phases continues with increased momentum into the third
and contemporary phase.

In the history of the Roman Catholic Church, these three
periods can be almost precisely dated. The first one begins
with the revival of Benedictine monasticism, following the
disruptions of the French Revolution. More specifically, it
can be dated from the refoundation of the Abbey of Solesmes
by Dom Prosper Guéranger in the year 1832. It reached its
culmination in the pontificate of Pius X, 1903–14, when the
movement entered a new phase of development under the
sponsorship of the papal authority. The boundary between
this second and the third, or contemporary, phase of the
movement is perhaps less clear. But it is fair to say that the
turn was taken, in the main, during World War II, or shortly
after the elevation to the papacy in 1939 of Pius XII.

Nowadays it seems to be a fashion among Roman Catholic
writers to disparage the work of Dom Guéranger. It is true
that his Benedictine revival and his liturgical interests were
largely colored by the romanticism of his age, in its strong
reaction to the ultra-rationalism and classicism of eighteenth-
century culture. Like all romanticists, he was more at home
in the piety of the Middle Ages than in that of the Patristic

age—and everyone knows, of course, that the medieval period was one of liturgical deterioration. It is true also that Dom Guéranger's excessive ultramontanism and his zealous campaign to suppress the relics of Gallican usages in the churches of France succeeded in imposing a rigid uniformity in liturgical practice. His scholarship lacked a critical discipline, and he was only moderately interested in making the liturgy available in the vernacular.

Nonetheless Dom Guéranger laid such foundations that without his pioneering the work of twentieth-century reformers would be impossible. One must remember that, however romantically conceived, however pressed into service for an ultramontanist program, his concern to restore the Roman rite in the purity of its text, ceremony, and chant was an essential starting point for any progressive work of reform. In particular, the glory of Solesmes has been its laborious and painstaking scholarship in the restoration of the ancient Gregorian chant. This work has been far more than an enrichment of our appreciation of the Western Church's cultural heritage. It has provided a fundamental insight into the true nature of liturgical song.

It was one of the surer pastoral instincts of Pope Pius X to begin the modern phase of liturgical renewal in the Roman Church by a call to reform the Church's music, on the basis of the Solesmes' achievements in the sphere of Gregorian chant. No proper liturgical spirit can develop among the faithful without an adequate vehicle of liturgical song. The fullness and perfection of the liturgy requires the choral participation of all the people of God. Christian worship, being pre-eminently eucharistic, must of necessity be realized at its best by a singing Church. It does not matter whether liturgical music is restricted to the use of ancient plainsong. Rather, the Gregorian chant is, as Pius said, 'the supreme model for sacred music.' One cannot exaggerate the profound influence that the Solesmes' achievements have had upon both the taste and the style of Church music in all Churches concerned with liturgical revival. The best of contemporary composers of Church music have all drunk deep from the well of plainchant melody, rhythm, and harmonic relationships, not to speak of its more indefinable spirituality. Wherever the Gregorian chant has been welcomed as a true model of liturgical song, there has been evident a wholesome reaction against Church music that is theatrical, sentimental, and trivial.

Nor should we forget that Dom Guéranger's work at Solesmes had a direct influence upon the extension of the Benedictine revival, in the latter part of the nineteenth century, in Germany, the Low countries, and England. If Solesmes concentrated upon research in the chant, these sister branches of Benedictinism did important pioneering in other areas of liturgical scholarship. The Beuron congregation in Germany, refounded in 1892, to which the distinguished Abbey of Maria Laach belongs, developed an interest in the 'mystery theology' of the sacraments that was destined to reach creative maturity and power of expression in our own times in the work of Dom Odo Casel—the most influential theologian of the Liturgical Movement to appear on the scene to date. The Belgian houses, and the English daughter of Solesmes at Farnborough, quickly took a leading place in liturgical studies through such publications as the *Revue Bénédictine* and the massive encyclopedia of Christian archaeology and liturgy edited by Dom Fernand Cabrol and Dom Henri Leclercq. The significance of such scholarly work, as these men promoted, lies in the new foundation that their studies laid for liturgical science, by shifting the base of liturgical enthusiasm from medieval to patristic standards. They thus took up once again the great work of seventeenth- and eighteenth-century Benedictines on the early Fathers—a work that had been interrupted by the devastating forces of the French Revolution—and in so doing they broke the spell that romanticism had cast about the new revival of liturgical interest in the nineteenth century.

The Benedictines were not the only ones, of course, who contributed to this vast development of historical research. One has only to mention the names of such men as Mgr. Louis Duchesne and Mgr. Pierre Batiffol to recall how great is our debt to non-monastic scholars of the Roman communion for the advancement of a scientific methodology in liturgical study. Nor were Roman Catholic scholars alone engaged in this work. Both the Anglican and Lutheran communions produced liturgical scholars of eminence, for these Churches were also engaged, by the latter part of the nineteenth century, in varying degrees of liturgical renascence. Exact scholarship is not bounded by ecclesiastical commitments. There is a community of scholars that transcends confessional loyalties. One of its signs was the foundation in 1890 of the Henry Bradshaw Society for the purpose of publishing important liturgical texts of all periods of Church history. To its work, scholars and libraries of all Christian communions have contributed. It is impossible to estimate what the Liturgical Movement owes to the pure and disinterested research of liturgiologists.

Liturgiology of itself, however, does not produce a Liturgical Movement. One cannot recount the history of the modern Liturgical Movement merely by way of a bibliographical guide to liturgical studies. Some of the most learned liturgiologists have had little concern about the practical applications of their historical findings, in the same way that certain scholars engaged in pure research in the natural and physical sciences feel no responsibility about the way that their theories, observations, and equations have been turned to advantage in inventions, whether for good or ill to human life. Many of the greatest scholars in the field of liturgics have spent their lives in academic or research institutions, for the most part separated from the responsibilities and actualities of pastoral work. If asked for an opinion about some particular liturgical usage they are likely to offer an idealistic solution based upon an historical precedent or norm. Liturgical reform often means to them little more than the restoration of some ancient text or custom in its pristine purity. One suspects that for this reason the Liturgical Movement has suffered, until recent years, from the charge of being archaeological and academic. Too many enthusiasts for liturgical reform have sought their inspiration from the liturgiologists.

The history of the reform of worship in the Reformation era should warn us that sudden and radical restorations of idealized past usages and norms do not revitalize liturgical life. If too drastic, they may impoverish it. Liturgical reform must develop from within a contemporary, living practice, however inadequate it may appear to the idealist and the scholar. It must work like leaven. It is, I believe, a fair judgment to say that the Anglican and some of the Lutheran reforms of worship in the sixteenth century have proved the more successful because of their more conservative character. They worked within the framework of the living liturgy of their time. The Churches that broke more radically with this tradition and suddenly introduced forms of corporate worship based upon the supposed practices of primitive Christian times, conceived as the ideal age of the Church's history, came near to losing all sense of liturgical worship altogether.

Similarly, in the modern Liturgical Movement, there has been a temptation to think that the mere restoration of supposedly correct liturgical usages, defined as correct by reference to some ancient or medieval norm, can produce a liturgical revival. Surely, Dom Guéranger's successful campaign in removing from the Church in France all the Gallican corruptions of the pure, classic Roman rite could never of itself have revived a true liturgical spirit in the Roman churches of that land. The Anglican Churches now know, from bitter experience, that the sudden restoration in the mid-nineteenth century of 'Gothic' norms for its liturgical practice, however much it may have enhanced piety in the Church, has not made more easy and effortless the enhancement of genuine corporate worship. And—one may be pardoned for saying so—the more recent imitations of Anglican public worship on the part of non-liturgically minded Protestant Churches here in America have for the most part only affected the externals of religion.

Having said all this, I return to reaffirm the importance of liturgiology, for its work is no less necessary. We cannot dispense with history, least of all with exact and scientific historical research. What is so heartening about it is the fact that it has achieved results of incalculable import. It has broken down thick walls of prejudice. No longer is liturgics studied with the apologetic aim of buttressing the separated structures of the Churches. An ecumenical atmosphere has been created in this field, and the several Churches of Western Christendom are more willing to be critical of their own usages and to learn from one another. Today there is a large consensus among liturgiologists of all Christian communions respecting the interpretation and evaluation of the history and development of the Church's public worship from New Testament times until the present.

Protestants listen today to what Roman Catholic interpreters, such as Romano Guardini, Joseph Jungmann, and Louis Bouyer, have to say about the liturgy, not merely because these men are prepared to admit that all is not well with the liturgical life of the great Latin Church, but chiefly because they speak to the central themes of our common Christian faith. On the other side, Roman Catholics respect the liturgical opinions of such scholars as the Lutheran Hans Lietzmann, the Anglican Gregory Dix, or the Reformed Oscar Cullmann, because these men seek to be honest with history, without special favor to their own ecclesiastical commitment, and because they build their liturgical reconstructions not narrowly, on the slender materials of the New Testament alone, but on the broader foundations of the whole patristic age of the great Fathers of the universal Church.

The second phase of liturgical renewal in the Roman Catholic Church dates, as already stated, from the official encyclicals and decrees of Pius X, beginning with the *Motu proprio* on Sacred Music published on November 22, 1903, just three months after his elevation to the papacy. This phase opened a vast program of education in liturgical principles, on the basis of Pius's directive that the 'foremost and indispensable fount' of a true Christian spirit and piety is 'the active participation' by all the faithful 'in the most holy mysteries and in the public and solemn prayer of the Church.' Specifically, the program launched by Pius X began with two major concerns: the restoration of Gregorian chant in its purity, and the stimulation of the faithful to more frequent communion within the context and celebration of the Mass. Pius also initiated a long-range revision of the official liturgical books, the fruit of which is only now, within the past decade, beginning to be realized.

Historians differ with regard to the exact time when Pius's directives began to be practically implemented. Dom Bouyer places it at the Catholic Congress in Malines in 1909, presided over by the famous Cardinal Mercier, when Dom Lambert

Beauduin of the Abbey of Mont César proposed the production of a vernacular Missal and the inauguration of retreats for parish choirs for the study of the chant.[1] In August 1911, the first Liturgical Week was held at Mont César, designed to interest the clergy in the study of the liturgy, and the production of translations of the Church's services. The Belgian monks also began at that time a series of semi-popular publications for the clergy, of which the most influential was Dom Beauduin's *La Pieté de l'Église* (1914).[2] This little book speaks of the official liturgy of the Church as 'the normal and infallible path to a solid piety.' In particular, he stressed the social character of the liturgy as the proper vehicle for uniting and sanctifying the faithful in the one mystical Body of Christ, thereby counteracting the individualism and secularism of the modern world. He also called attention to the teaching function of the liturgy, as the primary catechism of the Church for imparting the wholeness of Catholic truth and a corrective to the distortions and 'pious novelties' of much extra-liturgical devotion.

From its inception, the movement in Belgium had the ardent support of Cardinal Mercier and the hierarchy. At an early stage it formed a close alliance with Catholic Social Action groups. It was in Belgium that the first experiments were made with the so-called Dialogue Mass, a celebration of the liturgy in which the faithful join with the servers in active, audible participation in the responses and common chants of the Mass. The first International Liturgical Congress was held at Antwerp in 1930.

[1] L. Bouyer, *Liturgical Piety* (University of Notre Dame Press, 1955), p. 58.

[2] An English translation under the title *Liturgy, The Life of the Church* is available from the Liturgical Press of the monks of St. John's Abbey, Collegeville, Minnesota.

Almost contemporaneously with these activities in the Low Countries, the Benedictines of Maria Laach Abbey in Germany, under the leadership of their remarkable abbot Dom Ildefons Herwegen (d. 1946), inaugurated in Holy Week 1914 a Liturgical Week for laymen. By the close of World War I, the monks had launched an ambitious series of publications, at both the popular and the scholarly levels, treating all phases of the history, theology, and practice of liturgical worship. The popular series, called *Ecclesia Orans* ('The Praying Church'), began with the classic book of Romano Guardini, *Vom Geist der Liturgie*, which has been translated into many languages and remains the best single introduction to the meaning and purpose of liturgical worship.[3] It has converted untold numbers, both within and without the Roman communion, to active interest in the Liturgical Movement.

Two scholarly series sponsored by Maria Laach were the *Liturgiegeschichtliche Quellen und Forschungen* ('Sources and Studies in the History of Liturgy'), for the editing of ancient liturgical texts and the production of scientific monographs on historical, liturgical subjects, and the *Jahrbuch für Liturgiewissenschaft* ('Annual for Liturgical Research'), containing learned articles and an exhaustive, annotated bibliography of all publications in all languages in the field of liturgics. The editor of the latter series was Dom Odo Casel, whose significant articles adorned almost every volume. It is regrettable that to date Dom Casel's scattered articles and monographs have not been collected and translated. For they provide the most important single body of theological interpretation of the liturgy in modern times, and their influence has been felt far and wide. They have stimulated once more

[3] English translation by Ada Lane under the title, *The Spirit of the Liturgy* (Sheed and Ward, 1930).

creative discussion of sacramental theology in the Roman Church, such as has not been known since medieval scholasticism. Outside the bounds of the Roman Church, it may be sufficient to note Casel's influence upon such diverse scholars as Rudolf Otto, Gregory Dix, and Charles Harold Dodd.

It is impossible to do justice to Dom Casel's *Mysterientheologie* in a paragraph. He has infused into the arid scholasticism of official Roman dogma the fertile Platonic mysticism of the early Fathers. He has brought to bear upon the liturgical rites of Western Catholicism much of the spirit of Eastern Christian worship, and struck deep roots for them in both the Biblical faith and the sacramental experience of the whole Graeco-Roman world, where Christianity brought into a new, creative unity the finest insights and aspirations of the Jew and the Greek. The *Mysterium* of Christianity, as understood by Dom Casel, is not so much the content of the Christian revelation, to be apprehended by faith and explored by reason; it is the reality of redemption itself, the revelation of God Himself in Christ, in the totality of His mighty acts of incarnation, atonement, and exaltation, made present, operative, and effective in us through the participation of the body of the faithful in the cultic action of the liturgy. What God accomplished in Christ is made available to Christ's Body, the Church, through the liturgical mysteries.

Dr. Ernest B. Koenker has admirably summarized Dom Casel's position in this way:

In the liturgical rites of sacrifice and sacrament we meet the mystical making-present-again of the *totum opus redemptionis*; not only the Passion of Christ but his whole life, from the Incarnation to his Second Coming, is rendered sacramentally present in the cultic mysteries. It is not an empty commemoration or pious meditation; neither is this action something psychological or ethical. It is rather ontological action, a *signum efficax,* a reality which efficaciously heightens man's natural existence through an activity in a higher sphere; as such, of course, it works *ex opere operato*.[4]

Possibly the best translation of Casel's theology into English is Dom Gregory Dix's exposition of the *anamnesis* or 'memorial' in the Eucharist 'as meaning a "re-calling" or "re-presenting" of a thing in such a way that it is not so much regarded as being "absent," as itself *presently operative* by its effects.'[5]

Although Maria Laach has maintained its position as the leading center of inspiration of liturgical revival in Germany until the present, in the 1920's the movement found important foci of pastoral application in the work of Dr. Johannes Pinsk in Berlin and of the Oratorians in Leipzig; and in near-by Austria, in the remarkable teaching and writing of Dr. Pius Parsch (d. 1954) at Klosterneuburg, whose penny magazines *Lebe mit der Kirche* ('Live with the Church') and *Bible und Liturgie* ('Bible and Liturgy') had wide circulation. Guardini did valiant work in spreading the gospel of liturgical revival to the Catholic Youth Movement, until his activities were seriously restricted by the rise of Naziism. There developed in Germany, however, a number of excesses in bold experiments with the liturgy, beyond the bounds of what was canonically permissible, especially in the use of the vernacular. The German hierarchy was never solidly behind the movement, and it is reported that only Guardini's personal intervention prevented official condemnation.[6] The move-

---

[4] *The Liturgical Renaissance in the Roman Catholic Church* (University of Chicago Press, 1954), p. 107.

[5] *The Shape of the Liturgy* (Dacre Press, 1945), p. 245.

[6] Koenker, op. cit. pp. 18–19.

ment was set upon a more disciplined direction in 1940, when the German Bishops at their Fulda Conference set up a Liturgical Commission to regulate experiments and pass upon vernacular texts placed in the hands of the laity. With the appointment of this Commission—an action that has been imitated by the hierarchy in other European countries—the second phase of the Liturgical Movement may be said to have reached its climax.

Some account must be given, in this condensed survey, of what has happened in the United States. Again, the Benedictines took the initiative, notably St. John's Abbey in Collegeville, Minnesota, which inaugurated the periodical *Orate Fratres* (since 1951 known as *Worship*) in Advent 1925, and sponsored the first Liturgical Day at the Abbey in July 1929. Before the Benedictines became active in what they have always called the Liturgical Apostolate, the only significant work done in the Roman Church in America had been in the field of music, notably through the foundation in 1916 of the Pius X School of Liturgical Music at Manhattanville College of the Sacred Heart. In 1931 came the incorporation of the Liturgical Arts Society, whose quarterly has been a major contribution not only to the liturgical, but to the cultural education of American Catholicism. Both the Benedictine monthly and the *Liturgical Arts* quarterly have had extensive circulation—and one may add, healthy influence—among non-Roman Catholics. Indeed they have been the major American periodicals of influence upon all American Christians concerned with the Liturgical Movement. At Chicago in 1940, the first Liturgical Week was held, bringing together interested Roman Catholic clergy, religious, and laity from all over the country. This conference has been an annual affair ever since, with ever-widening participation and influence. In its initial phases, the movement in America had few supporters among the hierarchy. But this situation has now become quite the reverse, especially since the papacy has made its support unmistakably evident.

It is too early to assess the impact of the pontificate of Pius XII; but if his successor continues to pursue his policies, at least in the liturgical sphere, it will undoubtedly stand as a turning point in the history of modern Roman Catholicism.[7] Pius XII issued two encyclicals directly bearing on the liturgy: *Mystici Corporis* ('Of the Mystical Body') in 1943, an exposition of the doctrine of the Church, and *Mediator Dei* ('Mediator of God') in 1947, an interpretation of the liturgy itself. The latter is taken by the proponents of the Liturgical Movement as a very 'chart and compass,' though opponents of the movement have not been loath to point out the brakes this encyclical has placed upon certain experiments and practices. The motto of the encyclical might well be *Festina lente,* 'Make haste slowly.' But any fair-minded reading of this document makes evident the Pope's sincere support of the basic aims and many of the methods of Liturgical Movement leaders. Otherwise one cannot explain the extraordinary measures he has taken to reform liturgical practices. Before enumerating them, however, it may be of interest to quote the definition of liturgy in *Mediator Dei,* because of its comprehensive scope:[8]

The sacred liturgy is the public worship which our Redeemer as Head of the Church renders to the Father, as well as the worship which the community of the faithful renders to its Founder, and

[7] These words were written before Pius XII's death on October 9, 1958. Some indication of the outlook of his successor, John XXIII, concerning the liturgical revival is given in a report in *Worship* xxxiii (March 1959), pp. 252–4.

[8] I quote from the translation of Gerald Ellard, S.J., *On the Sacred Liturgy* (rev. ed.; The America Press, 1954), p. 20.

through Him to the heavenly Father. It is, in short, the worship rendered by the Mystical Body of Christ in the entirety of its Head and members.

The liturgical reforms of Pius XII began in 1945 with the issuance of a new Latin Psalter based upon a critical Hebrew text. The aim of this Psalter was to make possible for clergy and religious the recitation of the Daily Offices with understanding as well as with devotion. By 1950, the papacy began authorization—first in Germany, and since then in many other countries—of the use of the vernacular in the occasional offices of the Roman *Ritual*. Experiments initiated during the War with evening celebration of Mass have now been regularized, and with them has come a thorough revision of the canonical rules regarding the fast before communion. These changes have greatly facilitated the full participation of many of the laity in the Mass rite, especially those of the working classes. The most important of all reforms has been the revision of the Holy Week services and the restoration of the Easter Vigil. It was started on an experimental basis in 1951, and made permanently official in 1955. It is also known that reforms in the Calendar, the Breviary, and the Missal have been under consideration.

In connection with this last development, one must not overlook the International Study Weeks for Mass-Reform, of which the first was held at Maria Laach in 1951. These conferences have brought together the leading liturgical scholars of the Roman Church throughout the world, with prominent members of the hierarchy, to study the needs of changes in the Mass-rite. The findings of these conferences have been cordially received by the papacy. Indeed, since the third of these conferences, held at Lugano in 1953, the papacy has acted as sponsor of them, and has been represented by the presence and participation of several cardinals.[9] In the last few years, particular attention has been given to the problems of missionary dioceses in Africa and Asia because of the obstacles created by a Latin ritual. The demand for the vernacular in the Mass, at least for the audible parts, has now become a burning issue throughout the Roman Catholic Church. But to date the papacy has been loath to act except through cautious regulations for the Dialogue Mass.

In one area the Roman Church has taken such a revolutionary step (at least from our perspective) that it outweighs all other changes that have taken place: namely, the official encouragement now given to the faithful to use and study the Bible in the vernacular. This development is a direct result of the ferment of liturgical renewal. The new vernacular versions are both official and unofficial. Since the publication of the Latin Psalter in 1945, there have been published in this country alone at least one, sometimes three, English renderings every year bearing the imprimatur. The official translations being made in all Western countries are in the hands of the ablest Biblical scholars. We shall mention only two examples. The French version published under the direction of L'École Biblique de Jérusalem, and commonly known as the Bible of Jerusalem, is a marvel of scholarship

[9] The importance of these conferences deserves a more detailed listing: (1) Maria Laach, July 12–15, 1951, *Worship* xxvi (March 1952), 201–5; (2) Mt. Ste. Odile, near Strassburg, October 21–23, 1952, ibid. xxvii (February 1953), 149–53; (3) Lugano, September 14–18, 1953, ibid. xxvii (November 1953), 557–63; xxviii (December 1953), 28–9, and (February 1954), 116–20; (4) Louvain, September 12–16, 1954, ibid. xxviii (November 1954), 527–45; (5) Assisi-Rome, September 18–22, 1956, proceedings published as a supplement to *Worship* under the title *The Assisi Papers* (Collegeville: The Liturgical Press, 1957).

and, in addition, a thing of beauty. In the United States, the Episcopal Committee of the Confraternity of Sacred Doctrine is sponsoring the translation now in progress. The volumes that have appeared to date are scholarly, readable, and provided with enough notes and guides to make reading by the laity profitable and intelligible. The chairman of the sponsoring committee, until his lamented death in 1956, was Archbishop Edwin V. O'Hara of Kansas City, one of the most active leaders of the American hierarchy in the Liturgical Movement.

No one can foretell the ultimate effects of this new discovery of the Bible by the Roman Church. That it can only bring good, not only to that great Church but to all of Christendom, there can be no doubt. By letting loose the Word of God among the people, not merely willingly but also urgently, Pius XII has released spiritual forces of incalculable power. It is not likely that once so released, they can be controlled, much less recalled.

Some mention, at least, must be made of the Centre de Pastorale Liturgique ('Center of Liturgical Pastorate') founded near Paris in 1943 by the joint co-operation of the Benedictines, Dominicans, and Jesuits. No single agency in the Roman Church today combines and stimulates so many facets of liturgical revival. It publishes two periodicals: *La Maison-Dieu* ('God's House'), a magazine of unusual merit devoted to all phases of the liturgy, and *L'Art Sacré* ('Sacred Art'), a bimonthly on liturgical art. Through its publishing house (les Éditions du Cerf), have been issued a series called *Lex Orandi* ('The Law of Praying'), including both translations and original works, that is comparable to Maria Laach's *Ecclesia Orans*. Illustrated brochures (*Albums liturgiques*) on the several rites and seasons have also popularized the

movement.[10] Of especial importance has been the series
Sources Chrétiennes, editions of the early Fathers at popular
prices, prepared by outstanding patristic scholars, containing
the original texts with French translations, introductions, and
notes. To date over fifty volumes have appeared.

The French Center sponsors liturgical weeks, retreats,
workshops, and missions on the liturgy, and supervises the
issuance of vernacular texts of the rites under the direction
of the French hierarchy. Closely associated with the Center
have been the experiments in new methods of evangelization
of the industrial classes of France and of large numbers of
the lapsed, semi-pagan population of that supposedly Catholic country. This vast mission to France has become well
known to us through the work of Abbé Michonneau.[11] All
these developments in France have been fortunate in having
the strong and intelligent support of the hierarchy, most
notably of the late Cardinal Suhard of Paris.

The Non-Roman Western Churches

It is impossible to trace the history of liturgical renewal in
the non-Roman Churches of the West. What follows represents certain notes of obvious trends, and records the more
outstanding achievements.

In both the Lutheran and Calvinistic traditions, the liturgical revival has been chiefly concerned with the recovery of
liturgical norms produced in the Reformation era. Among

[10] English adaptations of these albums, the 'Fides Albums,' are being
issued by the Fides Publishers in Chicago. In format and scope they
are exactly similar to the French models.

[11] *Revolution in a City Parish* (Newman Press, 1949).

the Lutherans, it has been a reversal of the impact of Pietism. Among the Reformed bodies, it has been, at least in the English-speaking world, a reaction to the negative influences of Puritanism and of rationalism. In Methodism, there are stirrings of renewed interest in the modified Anglican rites given to it by the Wesleys. For the so-called free, non-liturgical traditions of the Congregationalists and Baptists, liturgical interests are still confined for the most part to the enthusiasm of individuals.

We would not dare to trespass upon the subject of Dr. Piepkorn's address, but say only this about the liturgical developments in modern Lutheranism. They began, as did those of Roman Catholicism and Anglicanism, in the nineteenth century with renewed interest in the *Kirchenordnungen* ('Church Orders') of Reformation times, which were revived and revised in a series of books known as *Agende*. The most influential of these was that of Wilhelm Loehe, *Agende für christliche Gemeinde* ('Liturgy for Christian Communities,' 1844). Loehe was a man of unusual spiritual gifts, not only as a liturgist but as pastor, preacher, counsellor, humanitarian, and missionary. His influence was felt in America. By the end of the nineteenth century the Lutherans had produced some of the outstanding liturgiologists, among whom mention might be made of Paul Drews. Concurrent with the development of liturgiological research, nineteenth-century Lutheranism recovered its magnificent tradition in Church music and chorale, as it culminated in the miraculous genius of J. S. Bach.

In more recent times, Lutheranism has given the Christian world some of its most stimulating and creative thinkers in the field of worship. One thinks of Rudolf Otto at Marburg, a philosopher and mystic and a Biblical critic of parts, whose *Idea of the Holy*, despite its subjectivism, has profoundly

affected our theological approach to worship. His liturgical
experiments were highly creative, though perhaps too
marked by his own individualism to be widely adopted.[12]
Contemporary with him in the 1920's at Marburg was Friedrich Heiler, a former Roman Catholic, leader of 'High
Church' Lutheranism, student of the psychology of worship,
but above all else an ecumenical spirit who greatly broad-
ened the sympathies of the Protestant world for traditions of
worship other than its own.[13] In the scholarly world, Hans
Lietzmann, a giant of Biblical and patristic learning, produced monographs on early Christian liturgy that have provoked and continue to stimulate research.[14] One must mention, too, Archbishop Yngve Brilioth of the Church of
Sweden, whose comprehensive analysis of the Eucharistic
rite in all periods of Church history has been esteemed by
Roman Catholics no less than Protestant churchmen.[15]

In the United States, the story of liturgical revival in

[12] *Das Heilige* first appeared in 1917; the English version, *The Idea
of the Holy* (Oxford, 1923; rev. ed., 1929), was followed by a 'supplement' in his *Religious Essays* (Oxford, 1931). Of special importance
is his *Zur Erneuerung und Ausgestaltung des Gottesdienst* (Giessen:
A. Töpelmann, 1925).

[13] His best known works, in English, are *The Spirit of Worship*
(Doran, 1926), and *Prayer, A Study in the History and Psychology of
Religion* (Oxford, 1932). Heiler planned a vast trilogy, of which two
volumes were completed—one on Roman Catholicism (*Katholizismus*,
1923), the other on the Eastern Churches (*Urkirche und Ostkirche*,
1937). The one on Protestantism was never finished. These works reveal
his combination of liturgical and ecumenical concern.

[14] The most important, *Messe und Herrenmahl* (1926), is now being
Englished by H. G. Reeve, with introduction and supplement by R. D.
Richardson as *Mass and Lord's Supper* (Leiden: E. J. Brill, 1954–).

[15] *Eucharistic Faith and Practice, Evangelical and Catholic*, translated by A. G. Hebert (S.P.C.K., 1930). Note especially the use of
Brilioth by L. Bouyer, op. cit. pp. 75ff.

Lutheranism can best be studied by marking the dates and comparing the Common Service Book of 1888 and the inter-synodical Service Book and Hymnal just published in 1958.[16] In the early years of our century, the Lutheran Liturgical Association, founded in 1898, did valiant work in promoting interest and published significant studies in the volumes of its *Memoirs*. Two liturgical societies were organized in 1932, that of St. Ambrose and another of St. James, the latter of which established in 1949 a Liturgical Institute at Valparaiso University. In the 1940's a group of Missouri Synod Lutherans began publication of an excellent liturgical periodical *Una Sancta*. All these groups, though relatively small, have brought before the Lutheran Churches reminders of the depth and richness both of their own and of other Christian heritages. The coming decades promise an extensive growth of liturgical concern in American Lutheranism; for it will come with the closer unity now developing among its separated pieces, since the cultural and linguistic differences of its several synods and organized bodies are no longer so divisive.

The Calvinistic Churches in Scotland and America have shown a development somewhat comparable to that of Lutheranism, although on a less extensive scale.[17] It began in the middle of the nineteenth century with a revival of concern for the standards of worship set forth in the Westminster *Directory* that had long fallen into neglect. The Church Service Society, formed in the Church of Scotland in 1865, published within two years a *Euchologion* that was widely

[16] The standard work is Luther D. Reed, *The Lutheran Liturgy* (Muhlenberg Press, 1947).

[17] See especially William D. Maxwell, *A History of Worship in the Church of Scotland* (Oxford, 1955).

adopted. Through the studies of this Society and its publication of early Reformed liturgies, interest was gradually aroused for a richer, more formal and more traditional type of public worship. By the 1920's the Church of Scotland was issuing new revisions of its historic orders of worship. The most recent edition of the Book of Common Order came out in 1940. Today some of the most creative experiments in corporate, Eucharistic worship are taking place in the Church of Scotland; and these are being enriched with a broader social consciousness through interaction with the Iona Community movement. The Church of Scotland has also given us several outstanding interpreters of the meaning of Christian worship, and of the sacraments in particular, in the writings of H. J. Wotherspoon, D. H. Hislop, D. M. Baillie, and W. D. Maxwell. Dr. Maxwell, especially, has devoted his scholarly studies to recalling the Scottish Church to the centrality of the Eucharist in the liturgical tradition that stems from Calvin's teaching and work.

In the United States, the turn to a richer liturgical life came to Presbyterianism by the pioneering studies of Charles W. Baird's *Eutaxia* in 1855 (recently republished as *Presbyterian Liturgies* by Baker Book House in 1957), and C. W. Shields' *The Presbyterian Book of Common Prayer* in 1864. These men were strongly embued with an ecumenical interest, though they lacked the depth and fervor of that extraordinary blossoming of theological and liturgical interest that flourished in the '40's and '50's at the German Reformed seminary in Mercersburg, Pennsylvania, under John W. Nevin and Philip Schaff. This Mercersburg Movement has yet to receive in American Protestantism the recognition it deserves.

By 1905, the Presbyterian Church (U.S.A.) had issued the first edition of its Book of Common Worship, under the

leadership of Dr. Henry Van Dyke and the famous hymnolo-
gist Dr. Louis F. Benson. Dr. Van Dyke also led the revision
of this liturgy in 1931. A third edition appeared in 1946. Each
successive revision of this book has shown an increasing debt
to the main stream of historical Christian liturgy, and a
closer approximation to the forms and content of recent
Anglican and Lutheran service books.

The Reformed Churches of Continental Europe are not
so advanced in liturgical revival as their brethren in Scotland
and America, though it is fair to say that they had wandered
less from the paths of classic Calvinistic rites.[18] A notable
liturgy was issued by the Reformed Church in France in
1948. Many have been fascinated by the novel experiments
of the monastic Reformed community of Taizé, with their
development of a 'reformed' type of Daily Office and liturgy.
Among the many curiosities of this group—though very exciting and healthy ones no less—are its happy relations with
the Roman Catholics, who allow these Protestant monks the
use of one of their parish churches for the community's
liturgical offices. The Swiss Reformed Church claims, in Dr.
Oscar Cullmann, a patristic and liturgical scholar like Lietzmann, whose studies of early Christian worship are held in
high regard by discerning students of all communions.

The Liturgical Movement in Anglicanism had its first
phase, as in other Churches, in the nineteenth century, as a
direct consequence of the conjunction of influence on the
one hand of romanticism, with its revival of interest in the
Middle Ages that expressed itself particularly in what is called
the 'Gothic revival' in art and architecture, and on the other
of the Oxford Movement, with its strong emphasis upon the

[18] A useful survey of developments in France and Switzerland will
be found in J.-D. Benoit, *Liturgical Renewal* (Student Christian
Movement Press, 1958).

sacramental life of the Church. The impact of these two forces changed not only the outward face of Anglican worship but also the temper of its inward piety. Unfortunately, the rather sudden introduction into many Anglican parishes of ceremonial usages and devotions from either medieval or modern Roman Catholicism provoked such heated and bitter controversy for over half a century that the tensions created thereby are still felt throughout the communion. It was unfortunate also that the zeal of the 'Ritualists' of that period, the more exasperated by unreasonable persecution from the Evangelicals, all too often developed their sacramental piety in an individualistic and emotional way. The estimate of them by Dom Louis Bouyer, a Roman Catholic, is not altogether unjust:

What the Anglo-Catholics of a hundred years ago were able to borrow from the Catholics of the time were precisely those features which now appear to Catholics to be among the weakest points in their recent liturgical practice. For example, a preference for low Mass (as private as possible) rather than a public celebration; the high Mass itself carried out so as to do without Communion or any participation at all by the faithful; and, above all, an enthusiasm for Benediction of the Blessed Sacrament which tended to make it, rather than the Mass itself, the focus of congregational worship.[19]

The Ritualistic controversy did, however, have advantageous effects. For one thing, it finally succeeded in breaking the rigid uniformity of Anglican worship that had bound it for over two centuries, and thus open to Anglicans both a more just appreciation of the comprehensiveness of their own tradition, and a wider experience of the fullness of Christian

[19] Op. cit. p. 48.

worship. It helped to open the eyes of Anglicans to the needs of 'all sorts and conditions of men,' who were repelled by the arid, overly intellectualized and formalized use of the Prayer Book into which the Anglican churches had largely withdrawn after the separation of dissenting bodies. Ritualism also fostered a new interest in the study of liturgiology. Though much of it was motivated by partisan and apologetic purposes, it did develop in the Anglican Communion scholars of pre-eminent reputation, such as F. E. Brightman, W. H. Frere, J. Wickham Legg, the Wordsworth brothers—John and Christopher—Bishop John Dowden (in Scotland), and Canon J. H. Srawley, to name but a few.

Ritualism also played a part in launching the second phase of liturgical revival in Anglicanism: namely, the generation of Prayer Book revision, which began with the American revision of 1892 and completed its first major round in the 1920's with the revisions in England, Scotland, Canada, South Africa, and a second revision in the United States. Other factors, of course, helped to bring about the revision movement—the stirrings of ecumenical interests such as Muhlenberg's Memorial Movement and the promotion of the Quadrilateral; the awakening in the Church of the social gospel and a wider missionary outreach; and not least the planting of Anglican missions overseas in cultures that were not even Western, much less Anglo-Saxon.

The whole period of Prayer Book revision from 1890 to 1930, to give approximate dates, was fructified by the tremendous advances made in liturgical knowledge in the nineteenth century. Naturally, the work of revision promoted among all the faithful a deeper knowledge and understanding of the history and significance of the Prayer Book liturgy. It made Anglicans consciously aware both of the strengths and the weaknesses of the Reformation settlement of worship.

It put a seal of acceptance upon a comprehensive diversity in Anglican worship: unity in essentials, permissible liberty in non-essentials. Anglicans can never again be so stuffy about their incomparable liturgy. Yet at the same time, they can evaluate with a surer conviction and reasonableness the remarkable heritage that is theirs in a liturgy both Catholic and evangelical, faithful to tradition yet alive to newer religious insights, a liturgy that can truly be an instrument of corporate participation in a language dignified and elevating yet no less understood by the people.

The third, or contemporary, phase of liturgical revival in Anglicanism began in the 1930's when the first great work of Prayer Book revision had come to completion. Actually, revision continues to go on, especially in younger provinces of the Anglican Communion, a continuing concern that bears promise of greater fruitfulness. But the peculiarities of the third phase are to be seen in the more intensive effort to relate liturgical practice to the pastoral, educational, and missionary life of the Church's parishes and missions. It is strongly influenced by both the developments of the Liturgical Movement in Roman Catholicism and the increasing encounters of Anglicanism in the Ecumenical Movement.

Pioneers of this third phase have been, in England, Fr. A. G. Hebert of the Society of the Sacred Mission, the late Dom Gregory Dix, and Bishops Henry de Candole and Colin Dunlop; and, in the United States, three scholars in their distinctive fields, all now deceased: Canon Winfred Douglas, who almost single-handedly reshaped the practice and taste of the Church in liturgical music; Professor Burton Scott Easton of the General Theological Seminary, whose massive learning in the New Testament and patristic fields richly interpreted the liturgical lectionary; and Dean William Palmer Ladd of the Berkeley Divinity School, the first person to popularize the Liturgical Movement in our Church and to point out its close relationship with the Ecumenical Movement, Christian social action, and a sound liturgical art. One might add the name of the late Professor Bayard H. Jones of Sewanee, but his contributions were more strictly in the classic discipline of historical liturgiology.

Since World War II, interest in the Liturgical Movement has gained considerable momentum in Anglicanism. Throughout the communion, the most obvious impact has been the rapid growth of what is called the 'Parish Eucharist' as the norm of worship on Sundays. This development has attempted to achieve three things in addition to restoring the Prayer Book (and ancient) ideal of Christian worship on Sundays. It has sought to reintegrate the worship of the Church through family participation. It has linked more closely to the Church's worship the Church's program of Christian education. It has reawakened many parishes—often through the help of its appended Agape, 'the coffee hour'—a greater sense of fellowship among Church people. Significant turns have been taken in the past decade with new forms of art and architecture, a breaking loose from the grip of taste for imitative styles of the past, particularly Gothic. Conferences innumerable, both for clergy and laity, now take place throughout the Anglican Churches on liturgical themes, or more specialized subjects such as Church music.

There is a great dearth still of good, popular literature on the liturgical revival coming out of Anglican circles, and no widely read periodical on the subject has yet seen the light. In England, the Parish and People Movement has made real progress in this area, and, on a much more limited scale in this country, the Associated Parishes. It is a curious circumstance that the religious Orders of Anglicanism have largely kept aloof, except for certain notable individuals, from deep involvement in the Liturgical Movement. And the theological seminaries, at least in America, though interested, are not zealously promoting the revival. Probably the real condition of the revival is indicated by the as yet untapped resources of Christian stewardship and the slender support given, as compared with other Christian bodies, to the Church's worldwide mission. Except for a relatively few people, the liturgical renewal in Anglicanism has not aroused an urgent sense of apostolate and of mission.

It is not possible to generalize the state of liturgical renewal in the free, non-liturgical Churches of Protestantism. Some individuals have made notable contributions. In 1936, a group of English Congregationalists published a valuable symposium on *Christian Worship*, edited by Dr. Nathaniel Micklem. One of the finest books on corporate worship yet produced in America was published as long ago as 1926, the late Dean Willard L. Sperry's *Reality in Worship*. Other volumes of distinction could be named, or such remarkable liturgies as those prepared by Dr. W. E. Orchard in *Divine Service*, prepared in 1919 when he was still a Congregationalist and long before his submission to the Roman Church.

The recent stirrings in the field of Biblical theology and the growth of the Ecumenical Movement will certainly combine forces to enhance liturgical interest throughout Protestantism. Since 1939 the Faith and Order sector of the Ecumenical Movement has had a Commission on Ways of Worship that has engaged leaders of all Churches, including several Roman Catholics on a voluntary basis, to exchange papers on the subject of liturgy. The Student Christian Movement has also promoted attention to the subject in its groups. There are now three Commissions on Ways of Worship at work—in Europe, North America, and the Far East—studying Christian worship at a much deeper theological level than has hitherto been the case. They are attempting to explore and explain the differences among the Churches not so much from the standpoint of their outward phenomena of worship, but from the basic theological presuppositions that underlie these outward expressions. To these discussions, the contributions of the Eastern Orthodox Churches have been of unique value. I cannot forbear from quoting a definition of the sacraments by the Russian churchman, Dr. Nicholas Zernov, in the Report of the Commission on Ways of Worship prepared for the World Conference at Lund in 1952:

The sacraments are the corporate actions of the Church which actualize the Kingdom of the Holy Trinity by uniting in Christ and regenerating their participants. They achieve this object by sanctifying the matter with the Grace of the Holy Ghost (water, bread, wine, oil, chrism) and by charging with the redeeming power social relations (community and individual, husband and wife, ruler and ruled).[20]

Just within the past year, two publication projects have been launched that will offer discussion of all facets of liturgical renewal by leaders of all Christian Churches. One is entitled 'Studies in Ministry and Worship,' under the editorship of Professor G. W. H. Lampe; the other, 'Ecumenical Studies in Worship,' directed by Professors J. G. Davies and A. Raymond George.

One must not conclude such a rapid survey of the liturgical revival without calling attention to the liturgy produced by the recently formed Church of South India. For this liturgy not only has an inherent excellence of its own, but it has proved beyond all expectation to be one of the most

[20] *Ways of Worship,* edited by P. Edwall, E. Hayman, and W. D. Maxwell (Harper, 1951), p. 31.

cohesive factors in melding together the varied traditions which combined to form that Church. Basically, this liturgy is a creative combination of Anglican and Calvinistic elements, with a salient admixture of borrowings from the Eastern Orthodox rites that relate it to the traditions of the ancient Eastern Churches of India. At the same time, there is gradually developing in the use of this liturgy an indigenous ceremonial and expression, what has been called the 'Indianization' of worship. The recent delegation of the Episcopal Church, which visited the Church of South India, reported of it:

We were impressed as we watched the C.S.I. Liturgical Committee at work both by their competence and their desire to blend the best of the tested historic forms of worship with natural Indian modes of worship. Already within the brief nine years in the life of the C.S.I. a liturgy has been developed in which there is a skillful fusion of elements borrowed from ancient Syrian, Anglican, Free Church, and Indian forms of worship. To be part of an Indian congregation praising God in a native tongue with characteristic vigor and enthusiasm is an unforgettable experience, which we were privileged to have in nearly every diocese we visited.[21]

Thus we should bear in mind that the future history of the liturgical renewal has much in store yet to be revealed, particularly as the younger Churches forming an independent life in Asia and Africa will doubtless have treasures to contribute to its ongoing development.

[21] *Report on South India,* Being Report of the Delegation to the Church of South India with Certain Recommendations and Theological Comments (New York: Joint Commission on Ecumenical Relations [1958]), p. 19.

III

THE PROTESTANT WORSHIP REVIVAL
AND THE LUTHERAN LITURGICAL MOVEMENT

The Reverend Arthur Carl Piepkorn, Ph.D.

*Professor of Systematic Theology,
Concordia Seminary*

THE PROTESTANT WORSHIP REVIVAL
AND THE LUTHERAN LITURGICAL MOVEMENT

The Protestant Worship Revival

IT IS fairly easy to characterize the liturgical movements in the communions that have a liturgical tradition. But it is not easy to reduce the worship revival in Protestantism to a single formula. One reason is the Protean and amorphous heterogeneity of Protestantism itself. Yet for roughly a generation there has been a worship revival in Protestantism. We can trace its growth in the series of quotations on the cover of the postwar pamphlet, *Seminars on Worship,* put out a decade ago by the Commission on Worship of the Federal Council of the Churches of Christ in America:

1925: All over the world today, men are beginning to re-think the place and purpose of public worship. This is the most hopeful sign on the religious horizon. (Willard L. Sperry)

1938: From Churches all over the world, both new and old, comes the report of a renewed interest in the approach to God through worship. (Madras Conference of the International Missionary Council)

1940: The Church must strengthen the spiritual resources of the people through prayer and public worship. In a day when hysteria and panic, depression and gloom, suspicion and hate are undermining the souls of men, the peace and power of God must become living realities. (Atlantic City Meeting of the Federal Council of Churches)

1942: There is a marked trend toward worship as the center of the life of the Church. This has shown itself in greater emphasis upon the development of the devotional life, and in the effort to make the public worship of God more beautiful and meaningful. (Cleveland Meeting of the Federal Council of Churches)

1944: Nothing in the Federal Council's program will call for as much emphasis as nourishing the spiritual resources of the people. (Samuel McCrea Cavert)

We see further evidence of this revival in the growing library of Protestant books on worship, including both discussions of the principles involved, and official and unofficial liturgies and books of corporate devotion.[1]

[1] Among early unofficial liturgies of merit there are S. Arthur Devan, *A Church Service Book* (Macmillan, 1924); W. P. Thirkield and O. Huckel, *Book of Common Worship* (Dutton, 1932); and James D. Morrison, *Minister's Service Book* (Willett, Clark and Co., 1937). More recently, note Boynton Merrill *et al.*, *A Book of Worship for Free Churches* (Oxford, 1948); and G. E. Osborn, *Christian Worship, A Service Book* (Christian Board of Education, 1953).

In 1942, Dean Willard L. Sperry and Dr. Henry Wilder Foote prepared an exhaustive bibliography, 'Public Worship,' published as a *Bulletin of the General Theological Library* (53 Mount Vernon St., Boston 9, Mass.), Vol. xxxv, No. 1. Any list of significant works would certainly include: Willard L. Sperry, *Reality in Worship* (Macmillan, 1925); John R. B. Sclater, *The Public Worship of God* (Doran, 1927); Von Ogden Vogt, *Art and Religion* (Yale University Press, 1921) and *Modern Worship* (Yale University Press, 1927); George W. Fiske, *The Recovery of Worship* (Macmillan, 1931); D. H. Hislop, *Our Heritage in Public Worship* (Scribners, 1935); Nathaniel Micklem (ed.), *Christian Worship* (Oxford, 1936); Andrew Blackwood, *The Fine Art of Public Worship* (Cokesbury Press, 1939); Albert W. Palmer, *The Art of Conducting Public Worship* (Macmillan, 1939); Scott Francis Brenner, *The Way of Worship* (Macmillan, 1944); Charles Heimsath, *The Genius of Public Worship* (Scribners, 1944); John R. Scotford, *The Church Beautiful* (Pilgrim Press, 1945); Henry Sloane Coffin,

Worship is perennially popular as a subject for magazine articles in Protestant religious journals, although no publication exists which could be called the organ of the Protestant worship revival in the sense in which *Worship* (formerly *Orate Fratres*) is an organ of the American Roman Catholic liturgical apostolate, or *Una Sancta* is an organ of the liturgical movement in the American Church of the Augsburg Confession.

The Department of Worship and the Fine Arts of the National Council of the Churches of Christ in the United States of America, with over twenty-five years of history of organic existence behind it, is very active under the leadership of its United Church of Christ Executive Director, Marvin P. Halverson. So are some denominational commissions on worship. Outside of such commissions, however, efforts at organizing the Protestant worship revival have usually had the fate of the short-lived Calvinist Catholic Society that Walter Lowrie tells us he organized during his student days at Princeton Theological Seminary.

In one sense, the return of ritual is a revolt against the exclusive intellectualism that traditionally marked the worship of Protestantism. 'When we contemplate the square,

---

The Public Worship of God (Westminster Press, 1946); Roger Hazelton, *The God We Worship* (Macmillan, 1946); William D. Maxwell, *An Outline of Christian Worship* (Oxford, 1936) and *Concerning Worship* (Oxford, 1948); Colin F. Miller, *Prayers for Parish Worship* (Oxford, 1948); the Protestant contributions to P. Edwall, Eric Hayman, and W. D. Maxwell (ed.), *Ways of Worship* (Harpers, 1951); J. Alan Kay, *The Nature of Christian Worship* (Philosophical Library, 1954); George Hedley, *Christian Worship* (Macmillan, 1953); Horton Davies, *Christian Worship: Its History and Meaning* (Religious Education Press, 1957); Raymond Abba, *Principles of Christian Worship* (Oxford, 1957); Douglas Horton, *The Meaning of Worship* (Harpers, 1959).

unadorned meeting houses of the Puritans and their stiff and formal service,' Methodist Bishop Thirkield wrote in the *Federal Council Bulletin* in 1932, 'it is almost with a shock that we learn, for example, of the wide sweep of liturgical reform in the Congregational Church.' He disclaimed the idea that the real question was one of ritual or of enrichment of the order of worship, and asserted that it was 'rather the securing of a sense of the presence of God in the service of the sanctuary. The lack of a spirit of orderly and devout conduct of the service and reverence in worship is a weakness in great numbers of our churches. Men crave to hear the note of eternity in the sanctuary.'[2]

A year earlier, George Walter Fiske, in his book *The Recovery of Worship*, which he described in a subtitle as 'a study of the crucial problem of the Protestant Churches,' had said in the same strain:

Many churches of the Puritan tradition have reached the point where they recognize the necessity of breaking with that tradition in its overemphasis on intellectual worship and its avoidance of the beautiful aids to worship. More beautiful churches, more worshipful music, more use of suggestive symbolism, the adoption of the chancel with its real aids to worship, the pageantry of the processional with the dignity of vestments, all furnish a vastly more psychological appeal to human worshipers, helping the service to appeal to the whole personality, instead of to intellect and conscience only. The greater the variety of channels by which the Spirit of God may find his way to the hearts of honest worshipers, the greater the likelihood that the worshiping soul will find in worship the Real Presence of the living God.[3]

---

[2] Wilbur P. Thirkield, 'The Sense of the Presence of God in Worship,' *Federal Council Bulletin* XV (April 1932), p. 10.

[3] Op. cit. pp. 233–4.

Here the theological is inextricably confounded with psychological considerations. This confusion is characteristic of the whole volume.

The worship revival received a related impulse from the reaction of Protestant Christians against the secularism and the insecurity of our times. 'The interest in worship,' an objective Protestant observer reported in 1945, 'is intensified by the present personal and social turmoil which leads people to seek the abiding and eternal. Worship furnishes the basic medium through which people become conscious of their "help in ages past," their "hope for years to come."'

The mere existence of effective worship in the Anglican and Lutheran communions has at every stage served as a stimulus to Protestant experimentation. W. E. Orchard, the 'Catholic' minister of the King's Weigh House Congregational Chapel in London, who later (1932) submitted to the Latin obedience, has cheerfully acknowledged this in his autobiographical *From Faith to Faith*. The influence of the Lutheran liturgiologist Luther Dotterer Reed on the Federal Council's Commission on Worship, and of Protestant Episcopal members of interdenominational theological faculties—Massey Hamilton Shepherd at the Divinity School of the University of Chicago, and Cyril C. Richardson at Union Theological Seminary in New York—can serve as American instances. In all honesty it must be admitted that the influence of Anglicanism has been generally stronger than that of the Lutheran Church.

It was not wholly an accident of history that the Protestant liturgical revival began in the 'twenties. The increasing wealth and leisure of the American people provided a congenial cultural soil for the aesthetic aspects of the movement. At the same time the general prosperity had taken the edge off the prophetic social witness that was a major part of the stock-in-trade of the creedless Protestant minister. The clarion call to build Jerusalem in America's green and pleasant land was an anachronism now that Jerusalem appeared to have been built. To many a liberal Protestant parson, liturgy seemed a providential replacement for the prophetic social message. A few saw this clearly at the time.

'Black Wednesday's' economic crash had not yet happened when Miles H. Krumbine, a Lutheran clergyman turned Congregationalist, wrote this perspicacious analysis:

Whether consciously or not, religion is giving itself to the erection of works amenable to the attitude of our times. It is institutionalizing the modern spirit and installing it within the portals of the Church. The first, and at this date perhaps the most visible, result is the widespread trend toward liturgy and liturgical practice that has overtaken religion. The trend to liturgy has much to commend it to our good sense. It may be our instinctive attempt to do something, not by way of preparation for doing something else, but for its very own sake. As such it may be a legitimate revolt against the philosophy of instrumentalism, as John Dewey calls it. By the widest stretch of the imagination, one can see no ulterior purpose being served by much of the modern liturgical practice. It is not designed to prepare us for something else; it exists for its own sake and for its own sake only. The thrill of the moment, the sense of interaction with reality that liturgy confers, is its only justification. It is worship, pure and undefiled. Setting aside its genesis and earlier implications, for many now it implies no preparation for work; it cherishes no illusion as to any possible usefulness. It is a process by which man transports himself to a realm of independent spiritual enjoyment and ecstasy. And while man carries with him into the secular world the mellowing consequences of the liturgical experience, those consequences stand in marked contrast to the secular experience. . . .

The supreme danger of liturgy is that, like the symbolist movement in literature, it will always tempt us to sacrifice truth to

effect; it will induce us to exploit the mysterious; it will put us
'more at home in Zion,' in the phrase of Carlyle, 'than any man has
a right to be.' . . . The fresh air and the glowing sunshine and
riotous color of the hillside by the lake dull the splendor of robes
and vestments no more than the dim light and vaulted arches of
the cathedral deaden the strident tones of the prophet. The age
of moral fervor is ending; the era of the aesthete has begun. The
raucous voice of the prophet must take on the soothing modula-
tion of the priest. The voice crying in the wilderness must somehow
manage to chant in a cathedral. The camel's hair shirt is giving
way to the silk gown, a much more agreeable garment.[4]

In part, the worship revival was a reaction as much against
crudity as against intellectualism. In the little six-page guide
to the *Symbolism in the Sanctuary* of the remodeled Franklin
Street Methodist Episcopal Church at Johnstown, Pennsylvania, rededicated on February 17, 1929, the author argues:

It ought not to be necessary to make any apology for beauty.
The late Prof. C. T. Winchester of Wesleyan University used to
say, 'If you get just beauty you get about the best thing God ever
made.' Now we are putting that beauty, the creation of God, into
God's house. The Reformation movement saved the religion of
Christ, not only for the Protestants, but also, through the counter-
reformation, for the [Roman] Catholics as well. But the Reformation leaders unnecessarily renounced beauty in doing it. Calvin's
little chapel in Geneva stands today as it stood in the height of his
work, as bare as the limbs of a winter-killed tree. They chose
between religion and beauty and they chose wisely. Perhaps in
their day the dilemma was necessary, but if ever necessary, it has
ceased to be so today, and exiled beauty is now returning to the
house of God. We have caught some of it here for the glory of
God, and are properly rejoicing in its possession.

[4] 'Are We To Have a Non-Moral Religion,' *The Atlantic Monthly*,
Vol. 144 (December 1929), pp. 823–4.

'There is no religious principle involved in the use or non-use of ritual, so long as it is the sincere expression of the worshiper's faith and experience.' So wrote George Walter Fiske in 1931.

Hence we find an astonishing amount of liturgy building now in nearly all nonliturgical denominations. Many have come to feel that slovenly extempore services are an insult to God; so several denominations have recently compiled and published their own prayer book and service book, not to be forced upon their congregations, but for voluntary use. And a generation of young people is growing up in these churches that is accustomed to the use of responsive, antiphonal material, accustomed to the reading of carefully prepared prayers, and to the planning of special worship programs with utmost care and devotion. With our present rate of progress in this matter of training in worship, another decade or two will make this matter of the use of ritual no longer a moot question.[5]

The prophecy has been fulfilled. In summer camps and conferences, in young people's organizations, in the worship services of schools and colleges, young people have been exposed to ordered worship and, especially where they have had a part in its preparation, they have responded enthusiastically. In the process a considerable quantity of good worship material for Sunday school and group use and a number of excellent youth hymnals have been produced for denominational and interdenominational use. It is not unfair to note that, in the tradition of American Protestant religious education, the emphasis is upon inspiration and aspiration rather than upon the expression of theological conviction.

Pragmatic reasoning had its part in encouraging the wor-

[5] Op. cit. pp. 70–71.

ship revival from the start. For example, Methodist Bishop Wilbur P. Thirkield wrote over a quarter of a century ago:

> In the report on additions to membership in the Protestant churches of Metropolitan Chicago for 1929 . . . it is rather startling to find that the increase in the Lutheran Church is greater than in the Presbyterian, Methodist Episcopal, Baptist and Congregational Churches combined . . . The Protestant Episcopal Church is next to the Lutheran. . . . Let it be borne in mind that the Lutheran Church holds to a liturgical service, to its evangelical doctrines, to the centrality of the Cross and of the Holy Sacrament, to catechetical training of youth, and to a definite creed.[6]

A cause-and-effect connection between the liturgical worship of the Roman Catholic Church and its apparent success in holding its own membership and attracting converts was frequently posited. 'An important urge expressed in the Protestant worship movement is the conviction that worship offers a timely means for revival of religion. The movement, except for certain fringes of idiosyncrasy, stems from a conviction that sincere worship issues in a strengthened and more devoted faith.'[7]

In some parts of Protestantism, the worship revival represented an effort on the part of the proponents of a liberal theology to find a proper liturgical expression for their beliefs. The Catholic creeds, the historic collects, the ancient prayer-forms, are all the expression of the Catholic faith of the historic Church. Mental reservations, recitation of the ancient forms in a 'historic' sense, glosses explaining away inconvenient doctrines, equivocating adaptations are in the

[6] Op. cit. p. 11.
[7] 'The Contemporary Worship Revival,' *Information Service*, XXIV, 39 (November 24, 1945), p. 1.

long run unsatisfactory. The problem for the extreme liberal in the Lutheran, Anglican, or Roman Catholic Church is ultimately solved by his withdrawal. In the Protestant denominations the problem was different. The inherited deposit of liturgical forms was limited, and in the general absence of liturgical prescription could be avoided. The task of creating an acceptable liturgy remained. The problem is set forth in considerable detail in Roger Hazelton's *The God We Worship* (1946), but it is faced peripherally by almost all of the more liberal Protestant writers on the subject.

The process actually antedated the Protestant worship revival in two areas—the construction of prayers and the writing of hymns. Walter Rauschenbusch published his *Prayers of the Social Awakening* in 1910, while in the field of hymns the names of John Greenleaf Whittier, Samuel Longfellow, Frederick L. Hosmer, Washington Gladden, William P. Merrill, and Frank Mason North come to mind.

The increasing preoccupation with beauty in the worship of God is likewise due, in part, simply to the rising cultural level of our whole society. There is a deeper appreciation of art in all its forms, and to the extent that this has affected the general level of taste it has set higher standards for worship to meet. Beauty is not sought as a substitute for sincerity, but sincerity is not regarded as an adequate excuse for crudity, although the thinking of liberal Protestant philosophers of worship has not always been particularly clear at this point.[8]

That an element of unadorned snobbery entered into the Protestant worship revival, a realistic appraisal must concede. Most communities have a kind of ecclesiastical 'pecking order' comparable to that of chicken yards. In many communities, the church that stands at the top of the list is the

---

[8] Cf. for instance, G .W. Fiske, op. cit. p. 147.

Protestant Episcopal Church. Americans have from colonial times undemocratically aped, even while they derided, their social 'betters,' and many an item of ritual was imported from the Anglican Church with the frank or covert justification that it was fashionable. That these features were sometimes precisely the things that well-informed Anglicans deplored in their own communion—processionals, recessionals, and mixed chancel choirs, are examples—is beside the point.

Another factor was unquestionably the decline of the oath-bound secret society as a respectable means of satisfying the American craving for pageantry. Older organizations, like Masonry, managed to maintain much of their ancient prestige. The more recent American imitations, however, with their anachronistic regalia and their extravagant titles came to be regarded as vaguely funny—the proper butt of cartoonist humor and the inspiration of the radio comedian. The minor lodges became to a greater and greater extent mutual insurance societies, and as the synthetic drama of the virtue-inculcating secret work played to fewer and fewer spectators in the lodge room, some of it found its way into the sanctuary of the church.

We may pause here to catalogue some of the major manifestations of the worship revival:

One of the more prominent phenomena was the so-called 'open' or 'divided' chancel. The Protestant tradition called for a pulpit-centered arrangement for the front of the church auditorium. Greatly daring, a number of 'advanced' parishes, in building and remodeling, began to substitute for this plan an imitation of the architecture of an Anglican church—with a communion rail open at the center, pulpit and lectern on opposite sides, choir stalls facing each other across the chancel, and an altar with a reredos or dossal curtain at the focus of attention. One of the first of this type in Methodism was the Franklin Street Church in Johnstown, Pennsylvania, to which we have already referred. In its guide, *Symbolism in the Sanctuary,* the congregation felt constrained to justify the rarity.

Typically, and quite contemporaneously, R. Claibourne Johnson describes a specific, though unnamed, Baptist church in this country, which he obviously would have us regard as an ideal church:

This church makes an extensive and effective use of symbols. The Communion Table, located at the rear of the chancel, takes the form of an altar. On it is a large open Bible brought into sharp focus by a special beam of light, flanked by lighted candles and flowers in brass vases. Behind and just above the Bible is a Celtic wooden cross against the background of contrasting colour. Over and above is a beautiful and lighted window, with the figure of the Christ with outstretched hands. Beneath that figure, unobtrusive and yet plain to see, are the words 'Come unto Me.' The ministers and choir are robed so as not to draw attention to themselves. The ministers wear Geneva gowns or academic robes which indicate a teaching and preaching rather than a priestly function. Pictorial glass and the use of symbols in appropriate recesses remind the worshipper of the great truths of the Christian gospel and of the facts of Christian history. The most liturgically-minded seem to feel at home, and yet those whose background of religious experience has been largely void of such things quickly appreciate the beauty and value of such a setting even for quiet meditation.[9]

The editor of the *Christian Observer* in 1912 concluded that 'the great Presbyterian churches which have so long stood as the bulwark of orthodoxy and simple worship have to all appearances abandoned the fight and are going over,

[9] *Ways of Worship*, ed. by P. Edwall, E. Hayman, and W. D. Maxwell (Harper, 1951), p. 145.

piece by piece, to Liberalism and ritualism.' The occasion for this jeremiad was the fact that in a 'conservative Presbyterian church,' which the editor had attended, the first Sabbath of April had been a celebration of Easter, a cross of flowers had occupied a central place on the pulpit, and a gowned choir of twenty-four voices had entered the church in stately procession and passed out (the phrase is his) singing the recessional hymn, while in other Presbyterian churches the Apostles' Creed was being recited.

A further phenomenon of the liturgical revival was the use of vestments, chiefly by the choir. At first, the choirs were usually 'robed' in discreet black, with white Buster Brown collars for contrast, and on the women, sometimes, a mortarboard, a Canterbury cap, or a coif. White surplices followed in many places. As the idea caught on, the religious supply catalogue houses, with no traditional liturgical standards to trammel them, had a field day, each vying with the other in producing more colorful surplices, capes, hoods, and even stoles, in every shade of the spectrum. The clergy had recourse to academic gowns, together with the ornaments and hoods of their earned or honorary degrees. Occasionally but increasingly, Methodist clergymen, claiming the privilege of their Anglican heritage, and even Congregationalists, donned surplice and, more rarely, even a plain stole. Though a clergyman might not wear the surplice at ordinary services, he might do so when solemnizing a wedding.

Back in the seventeenth century, John Endecott, the zealous governor of the Massachusetts Bay Colony, felt impelled to cut the cross out of the British flag flying over the State House in Boston, not because he loved England less, but because the cross was to his Pilgrim conscience the hated symbol of all the tyranny and the detestable enormities of the Bishop of Rome. The cordial acceptance of symbolism by the Protestant worship revival accordingly stands as a considerable *volte-face*. Sometimes it was restrained, as in the lovely Memorial Chapel in the Yard at Harvard, with its discreet cross over the screen that separates the Appleton Chapel from the main church, and its barely distinguishable symbols in the capitals of every other column high above the nave—the four traditional symbols of the holy Evangelists, the pelican-in-her-piety, the Agnus Dei, and the ascending and descending dove. Sometimes the acceptance was nothing less than exuberant. In the Franklin Street Methodist Church at Johnstown, for instance, the guide to the symbolism of the sanctuary included, in addition to the frankly symbolic architecture, the bursting pomegranate of the Resurrection; the thistle of human sinfulness; the Messianic rose; the head of wheat (interpreted as the Seed of the Word); the Patriarchal cross (for Calvary) entwined by the serpent of sin and accompanied by the crossed keys significant of forgiveness; the Alpha and Omega; the cross of the atonement; the fleur-de-lys symbolizing the human nature of our Lord; the vine-and-wheat motif; a Maltese cross for St. John the Baptist on the font; the four Evangelists' symbols; the fish; eight shields with symbols of the Passion; and the name of a disciple in each of the twelve sections of the communion rail. ('Even Judas is included, and we cannot but believe that our forgiving Master would have it so.') Such a mass of symbols, carefully but briefly explained in the little guide, ultimately conveys an impressive quantity of theological knowledge.

A fourth area where the worship revival had a pronounced effect was in the realm of Church music. The Hymn Society of America, while not exclusively Protestant, is predominantly so; its history from its founding in May 1922 is roughly co-extensive with the era of the Protestant worship revival. The same three and a half decades have seen the publication of a

very considerable number of Protestant hymnals and hand-
books, some of them of outstanding merit.

Theologically significant in this vast hymnological produc-
tivity is the increase in the number of hymns of worship and
the decline in the number of hymns preoccupied with subjective and personal piety; a growing number of hymns re-
vealing a social awareness, a non-nationalistic patriotism, and
a yearning for peace in our time; an eschatological orientation
that thinks in terms of personal relationships and self-forget-
fulness in the service of God; and increased emphasis upon
God as Creator and less emphasis upon God as Redeemer;
the excision of descriptions of the physical agonies of our
Lord's Passion in favor of spiritual interpretations of His
sacrifice; a tendency to eliminate such doctrines as original
sin and the eternity of hell; more frequent reference to God's
providence, mercy, and goodness, and less frequent reference
to the Trinity in Unity, God's sovereignty, and God's im-
manence; a decreasing evangelistic emphasis; more hymns
on the Holy Spirit, on Christ's humanity, His Resurrection,
and His fellowship with men, fewer on the atonement and
our Lord's Godhead; sin described in social terms rather than
as individual depravity; a decrease in motives of fear and
awe and an increase in motives of love, gratitude, and fullness
of life.

In 1926, the Westminster Choir College came into being.
The Union Theological Seminary School of Sacred Music
was organized in 1928. Both have been the inspiration for
many other schools and departments of sacred music in
colleges and universities. As a result, the quality of Church
music in American Protestantism is notably higher today than
it was a generation ago. Evidence of this improvement lies in
the increasing number of professionally trained, full-time
ministers of music, in the vogue enjoyed by the good com-

posers both contemporary and classic, from Schuetz, Buxte-hude, Bach, and Palestrina, to Ralph Vaughan Williams and Healey Willan, and in the sturdy and solid growth of the Protestant element in the American Guild of Organists.

The fifth significant development is the recovery of the Church Year. The gradual introduction of the major holy days, first Easter, then Christmas, Pentecost, Holy Week, and Lent, is a commonplace of the history of Protestant worship in this country. The general observance of Good Friday is traceable to the efforts of the San Francisco Joint Committee for the Reverent Observance of Good Friday in 1914. Toledo, Indianapolis, Duluth, and Philadelphia, followed in the 'twenties. By 1937 the movement had progressed to the point where the Federal Council's Commission on Worship, under the leadership of Fred Winslow Adams, published the first edition of the pamphlet, *The Christian Year*. It endeavored to combine the traditional seasons and days of the liturgical tradition with special days inspired by contemporary inter-ests. Contemporary needs and concerns displaced all but the most reverend of the ancient commemorations; at the same time, a significant step was taken toward a common unified program that made for a greater sense of community across denominational lines. Less distinctively Protestant and more authentically ecumenical are the efforts of the National Council of the Churches of Christ Committee on the Chris-tian Year, whose work is still in process.

Of course, Protestants have not accepted these changes and innovations either universally or unprotestingly. 'Enthusias-tic' groups have consistently regarded the ordered worship of the worship revival as a quenching of the Spirit and have criti-cized it vocally in the terms which they previously reserved for Roman Catholics, Anglicans, and Lutherans. Among more conservative groups the reluctance to adopt what in childhood they were taught to be popish traditions has been very strong.[10] The Federal (now superseded by the National) Council's sponsorship of the worship revival has proved to be a liability in those areas where the Federal Council has been equated with the fountainhead of religious, political, and economic liberalism. Communities that have not been deeply affected by the rising cultural level of the country actually prefer the excitement of completely spontaneous worship and revel in what more sophisticated groups regard as crudities.

Some of these factors are pointed up in the summary of an address which J. N. R. Score delivered on 'Worship in the Southwest' in 1946:

The average church has one room, or two, or three, without benefit of architecture and without benefit of either the atmosphere or understanding of worship. The average pulpit is still the Chautauqua platform, often used as a propaganda agency for denominational programs. In such a situation worship suffers. It is regarded still as 'opening exercise.' The life of the churches of the Southwest is marked by an intense independence. They want to run their own show and do not want assistance from New York or the bishop [Dr. Score speaks as a Methodist] or the denominational headquarters. There is a distrust of prepared services of worship material and other aids to the worshipful approach to God. Informality is exalted and people are unmindful that 'the formality of informality is the greatest formality.' Certain informal groups, such as the singing fests, militate against reverent worship. Out of 200 Methodist churches with which I am in touch, I think 150 have no pulpit Bible. We have difficulty in the field of worship with untrained and overenthusiastic ministers who are devoted to this subject. . . . The general mind of the church in the Southwest is not yet for better worship.

[10] A notably articulate exposition of this position is Ilion T. Jones, *A Historical Approach to Evangelical Worship* (Abingdon, 1954).

From another point of view, Morgan P. Noyes has stated:

Still another difficulty with a liturgy that is fixed by canon law is that it is often couched in a theological vocabulary quite at variance with everything that a church does and quite at variance with the known beliefs of the minister who reads the words. . . . The Prayer Book Communion Service is to a great extent in the vocabulary of a substitutionary doctrine of the atonement not held by many Episcopal ministers of my acquaintance. But that is what they have to read at the altar.[11]

The presence of an 'open chancel' has been no guarantee that it would be properly used. In one such church, the new minister ignored the pulpit and preached from the lectern the first few weeks; then he took the Bible into the pulpit and ignored the lectern. The altar he ignored all the time. He introduced a self-service Communion set and knelt inside the chancel rail facing the congregation for all the prayers. In another church, the new minister in his second week moved the pulpit in front of the altar, concealed the latter with some old pulpit chairs, and used it as a stand for some books and a small clock. In a third, the new minister put a pitcher of water and two glasses on the altar, conducted the first part of the service from a choir stall, read the Scripture and offered prayer from the lectern, introduced the speaker from the pulpit, and announced the last hymn and pronounced the benediction from one of the pews. A liturgical minister built a congregation up from twenty-five to sixty-six members in three years; a non-liturgical man reduced it to fifteen in a year. Another built up a service averaging forty-five worship-

11 'Worship in the Reformed Tradition,' *Anglican Theological Review* XXIX (1947), 224.

ers to an average of ninety-three in four years; a non-liturgical man brought it down to forty.[12]

Another factor that has promoted the worship revival in Protestantism is the growing ecumenical interest. Association of churches in local church federations, and of denominations in the Federal Council, thrust into close proximity groups and individuals of diverse worship traditions. Serbian Orthodox and Nazarene Christians came to know one another; Protestant Episcopal churchmen and members of the Church of God; Swedish Augustana and United Lutherans and Disciples of Christ. Curiosity about the others' religious life extended to dogma and worship as well as to practical methods of church work. The liturgical have-not denominations discovered that certain worship needs could be met adequately without imitating the Roman Catholic Church, simply by learning from fellow-evangelicals.

This civilian experience was reinforced in both wars—notably in World War II—by the experience of both laymen and clergymen in the military service. This enforced association was welcomed, or at least not resisted, among most non-liturgical Protestants. Some of the non-liturgical chaplains felt an acute concern about ministering to the Lutheran and Protestant Episcopal men in their organization. Many of them were honestly unable to appreciate the fundamental theological differences that separate Lutherans and Anglicans from Protestants, and tended to regard the difference as being primarily one of rite and worship. With the best of intentions they imported elements from the Common Service Book and the Book of Common Prayer into their Protestant services. Here and there the response of Lutherans and Anglicans,

[12] William Esler Slocum, 'The Coming Revival,' *The Brotherhood of St. Luke,* pp. 7–8.

whose inadequate religious training led them to be guided by superficial externals, encouraged the chaplains in their procedure. In other cases, the response of the non-liturgical Protestants in the congregation to a dignified service, even though it leaned heavily on Lutheran and Anglican liturgical materials, served as further encouragement.

The wartime chapels of the Army and the Air Force were meticulously neutral in basic design. Since, however, the Roman Catholic Mass was said daily in most chapels, whereas the Protestant services tended to be restricted to Sundays and Wednesdays, sheer inertia operated to keep the altar pulled out into the chancel. Quite inadvertently, reredoses, dossals, and carpets were so installed that while it was still physically possible to push the altar into the wall and center the pulpit, the aesthetic consequences tended to militate against the arrangement. Very doggedly, antiliturgical chaplains carefully removed the cross and candlesticks from the altar, but most of them were content to replace the crucifix of the Lutheran and Roman Catholic service with a cross and to light all the candles in sight. By the end of most Protestant chaplains' tours of active duty, they had become quite habituated to altar, cross, and candles. So had their congregations.

Viewed from the technical angle of worship, some of the devotional booklets prepared for use of service-people furnished admirably conceived and devised materials for both group and private worship. Among them should be noted the *Spiritual Almanac for Service Men* of the Federal Council's Commission on Worship, the Methodist *Strength for Service to God and Country*, and the Y.M.C.A.'s *A Book of Prayers for the Armed Forces*.

In civilian communities, the growing vogue of community and interdenominational services necessitated fixed orders of service the moment that they rose above the level of religious exercises. As long as informality was regulated by parochial or denominational tradition (and the control of such tradition is actually very strong), services within a congregation or a denomination needed only to conform to the pattern. But only few experiences clearly indicated that in the absence of such control informality was a mortal enemy of effective worship, and so a fairly rigid order of service tended to be devised in order to protect both the officiants and the congregation.

The great World Conferences of Lausanne, Stockholm, Oxford, Edinburgh, Madras, Oslo, and Amsterdam, and more recently Lund and Evanston, gave great impetus to this development. In each case the worship services were a major center of interest, and were almost invariably reported on most favorably by the participants. For 'communities which want to make the best use of "union" services or special occasions of worship in the interest of unity,' the American office of the World Council of Churches developed and published a little *Primer of Ecumenical Worship*. A special order for a 'Service of Ecumenical Worship' represents a concrete application of the principles set forth in the *Primer*.

Another factor that has given an interdenominational stimulus to the worship revival is the rise of the community church, both the undenominational and the denominationally affiliated kind. In drawing individuals of a great variety of backgrounds together in a reasonably permanent association —in contrast to the transient and accidental congregations of the military service—the ministers of these churches have usually sought to incorporate the worship traditions of as many denominations as possible in their services.

As yet another factor, we may list the awakening of a historical consciousness. Denominations whose worship development was in a non-liturgical direction have found that this lack of liturgical concern was not a necessary concomitant of their theology.

There is a growing desire to recover elements in the Christian heritage which were discarded at the time of the Reformation. In the general church house-cleaning of that time, many worthy and deeply significant worship practices were given up. Gradually these are being reinstated.

The present new appreciation of the Church 'as Church' carries with it a growing regard for the worship practices which have long marked its life. The influence of the years is felt in this return to those expressions which have the authority of centuries of Christian experience.[13]

This has been particularly true in the Churches of the Calvinist tradition. The Reformed Church of Germany and its American offshoot retained at least a rudimentary Church Year and such historic features as the Epistle and Gospel. This was true, incidentally, of the German Mennonites also. In Scotland, there have been many signs of a liturgical revival: the Iona Community under George MacLeod's direction; the publication of the Church of Scotland's interesting liturgy in 1940; the solid historical research of William D. Maxwell into both ancient and Reformed liturgical development; and the appearance of Colin Miller's *Prayers for Public Worship*. In the United States, the Presbyterian Church in the U.S.A. published a new edition of its *Book of Common Worship* in 1946, which contained many changes; and even the very conservative Presbyterian Church in the U.S. (the 'Southern' Presbyterian Church) has not been wholly without a liturgical tradition.

[13] Art. cit. note 6.

The Liturgical Movement has made little headway in Zwinglian Switzerland, but elsewhere on the Continent the revival of liturgical interest in Reformed circles has produced such interesting phenomena as the French Calvinist monastery at Taizé (The Evangelical Reformed Community of Cluny) and its associated sisterhood at Grandchamp, Switzerland. Calvinist in its theology, the order has combined elements from the Rules of St. Francis and St. Benedict in its rule. Members are pledged to celibacy, obedience, and poverty; they engage in manual labor, so that the community is self-supporting; in meditation and worship; in study and writing; and in charitable activity, particularly among war orphans.

In some respects the worship revival in the Methodist Church has set the pace for American Protestantism. The Methodist Church's *Book of Worship* (1945) is an important and ambitious document, both because of the wealth of orders of public worship and because of the wide variety of additional material, notably for private and family devotion. Noteworthy in the Methodist rite are the encouragement for the congregation to kneel at many points in the service, the use of silence, and the recommendation of the *Venite* or *Te Deum* as the anthem or chant.[14] The historic tie with the Church of England, from which the Wesleyan movement went forth, is being recalled as justification for the use of services closely related to and extensively dependent on the Book of Common Prayer.

In the Methodist Church a liturgical society sprang into being in 1946 as the result of articles written for *The Pastor*, a Methodist clergy journal, by William Esler Slocum and

---

[14] *Time* (April 25, 1932) took cognizance of this departure with a half-column story headed 'Methodist Kneel.'

R. P. Marshall. Slocum's interest lay in the field of Christian healing and mental hygiene; Marshall's concern was more exclusively in the area of liturgy. These factors determined the name, the Brotherhood (later the Order) of St. Luke.

According to the historical statement, the rule of the Brotherhood stresses magnifying the place of the sacraments (a monthly Eucharist as a minimum and Holy Baptism as the act whereby candidates are admitted to the Kingdom of God); adherence to the *Book of Worship* in the conduct of divine service; use of the ceremony of Reception into Full Membership (formerly called Confirmation), preceded by instruction classes; the cure of souls (including evangelism without revivalism); systematic private devotions for the clergy (which some of the members extend to include a daily celebration of Holy Communion *devotionis causa*); wearing of clerical garb (except where it would mean misunderstanding and persecution) to include clerical collar for street wear and at least a pulpit gown, and a cassock, surplice and stole, if possible, for service use and at weddings and funerals; and loyalty to the Methodist Church. The Brotherhood's general theological statement pledges the members

to uphold the theological statements contained in the Great Ecumenical Creeds of the Councils of the Undivided Church, namely The Apostles' and The Nicene. The theological statements of these creeds constitute orthodoxy. These truths are explained in the Articles of Religion of The Methodist Church.

The Mission Covenant Church—formed when the Waldenströmian schism separated from the Swedish Lutheran Augustana Synod—has a group which is acutely conscious of the Lutheran background of the denomination and which retains as much of the Lutheran liturgical and doctrinal heritage as possible.

The Moravian Church (*Unitas Fratrum*) has a liturgical tradition that antedates the Reformation. In recent years the American branch of the Church has produced a well-received and distinctive *Hymnal and Liturgies* in 1924, and the *Moravian Youth Hymnal* in 1942.

The United Church of Canada produced a most interesting and thoroughly historical liturgy in 1932.

A further factor that has encouraged the worship revival is the perennial Protestant desire to cultivate the devout life. It will be remembered that the Wesleyan revival began with the ordered devotions of the Holy Club at Oxford. Associated with the worship revival in Protestantism in our time is a reviving interest in the great contemplatives in the history of Christian devotion: the anonymous authors of the *Imitation of Christ,* the *Cloud of Unknowing,* and the *Theologia Germanica* (which Blessed Martin Luther published in his century); Brother Lawrence; St. Francis de Sales; François Fénelon; St. Augustine; and others.

A reviving interest in social problems has also made its contribution to the worship revival. Its genesis in Walter Rauschenbusch's *Prayers of the Social Awakening* (1910), we have already noted. In this context, Charles Clayton Morrison wrote *The Social Gospel and the Christian Cultus* (Harper, 1933). It has found expression in the programmatic relation of worship to rural church work by a number of interdenominational agencies. Part of the association of worship with a social concern may be traceable to persistence of this pattern in the Anglo-Catholic revival. This emphasis is apparent especially in the orders of service prepared by denominational and interdenominational agencies for use on Thanksgiving Day, World Order Day, Race Relations Sunday, Labor Sunday, and similar occasions.

By way of summary, we can begin with the informal

statement made by Marvin Halverson when he became Executive Director of the National Council's Department of Worship and the Fine Arts. In outlining the Department's plans,

he suggested extending the study of worship in additional directions, citing 'A Common Language' by Denis de Rougemont which refers to the profound issue to be explored. The relationship of life and witness of churches can be examined with profit. The theological dimension is necessary in study of historic and contemporary liturgies.[15]

We have seen that the Protestant worship revival has resulted from a variety of factors, with both theological and non-theological implications. We cannot account for it by any simple formula.

In part, it is a reaction against an almost exclusive intellectualism. This may be a revolt against theology *per se* or merely against irrelevant theology that has lost significance for the life of the people. In some cases, the worship revival may be an effort to find in the psychologically related area of aesthetic experience a substitute for a lost radiance of personal faith. In other cases, the worship revival is a legitimate effort to find a more comprehensive approach of the past contemplated. In such cases, no sacrifice of theological principle is involved and the total response to the combined avenues of approach to the individual results in a deeper and more potent faith.

We have seen that the worship revival is a reaction against secularism and insecurity. Where it is subjective escapism, it represents a theological loss. Where it is an objective com-

---

[15] Minutes of the Meeting of the Department of Worship and the Fine Arts, National Council of Churches, New York, May 1, 1952, p. 2.

mitment to the God whose mercy endureth for ever, it gives evidence of a deepened theological insight and faith.

Insofar as the worship revival is related to the general rise in cultural level in our country, it is theologically significant only insofar as the changing cultural pattern, with its emphasis on things, is in its totality theologically significant.

Where the new worship patterns are an effort to give liturgical form to new tenets and theological opinions, they are vitally significant and deserve study. St. Celestine's principle, *lex orandi lex credendi*, is still valid. A modern Protestant theologian asserts: 'Worship is dogma come to life. . . . If the liturgical movement has anything to say it is this: Christian worship is a bringing near and an acting out of Christian faith and belief.'[16]

The Protestant reaction to the worship revival has not generally been on grounds that are theologically meaningful. Supporters of the social gospel have complained that the worship revival is a substitute for a genuinely prophetic social message; it may merely signalize the fundamental theological bankruptcy of the optimism about human capabilities that underlay the modern social gospel. It is not amiss to point out that all the authentic liturgical movements of the nineteenth and twentieth centuries, regardless of denomination, have been accompanied by an increased emphasis upon Biblical preaching and study of the sacred Scriptures. This is simply a reflection of the actual integral relationship of the means of grace; genuine concern for the sacred Scriptures and genuine concern for the sacraments go together.

We have seen that the increasing ecumenical interest can be related to the worship revival. Where the Ecumenical Movement is simply the organizational expression of a prag-

[16] Howard G. Hagemann, 'The Liturgical Revival,' *Theology Today* VI (1950), p. 500.

matic lust for bigness, for bigness' sake or power's sake, the theological significance which it contributes to the worship revival is baleful. Where a solid theological consideration of the nature of the Church underlies the ecumenical interest, the worship revival is a tool to better understanding of the theological and non-theological factors involved.

Where a growing historical consciousness has affected the worship revival, it has been accompanied by a deepened interest in the historical creedal position. Since many of the denominations concerned entertained strong creedal convictions in the past, this new interest represents a net theological gain. It would be inaccurate to say that the worship revival has produced the creedal interest or *vice versa;* both have unquestionably reinforced each other.

The devotional concern as a factor in the worship revival stresses theologically less significant elements. The emphasis is more likely to be on the mystical side. This may be a warm, welcome, and appealing complement to a theologian's makeup; it may also be subjective and theologically negative, particularly when it veers in the direction of a besetting pantheism.

The Lutheran Liturgical Movement

In more ways than one, we could say that the Liturgical Movement in the Church of the Augsburg Confession began in the sixteenth century. The Reformation itself, in its immediate homiletical, liturgical, ecclesiological, and sacramental goals, and in its eschatological emphasis, was a liturgical movement. It sought to restore to the pulpit the consistent communication of the gospel of a gracious God in Christ Jesus. It sought to give practical and palpable expression to its conviction that the Church is not merely an external association, but first and foremost the Body of Christ, an effective brotherhood of men bound together by a common faith in the incarnate Son of God as Lord and Saviour, a social process through which the Holy Ghost works among men, extending backward in time to our first parents and forward in time to the ever-imminent close of the age. It sought to restore the public worship to the whole congregation. It sought to restore to their proper place in the life of the Christian and of the Christian community the sacraments of Holy Baptism, Holy Absolution, and Holy Communion. The first generation of reformers anticipated that the Parousia would come in the sixteenth century. Although that hope failed to materialize, the Reformation succeeded, in varying degrees, in realizing its objectives for at least a century and a half. But finally pressures from without and decay from within robbed it of the major part of its effectiveness.

The cumulative reaction to these forces of decay and destruction produced the German Lutheran liturgical movement of the nineteenth century, with which the names of Loehe, Kliefoth, and Vilmar are inseparably associated. The appeal of these men was significantly to the principles of the Symbolical Books of the Lutheran Church. The influence of these men was not limited to Europe. Their concern for the Lutheran missions in America, their personal contacts, and their writings bore tangible fruit in the Lutheran Common Service of 1888 and in the influential liturgical writings of Friedrich Lochner.

Various circumstances conspired to limit the effectiveness of the nineteenth-century Lutheran liturgical movement in Europe itself. The rationalism and humanism in the Church, against which the liturgical movement was a protest, took strength from the scientific and philosophical doctrines of the latter nineteenth century and achieved an apparently all but complete triumph during the optimistic years at the turn of the century.

The disillusionment that followed World War I ushered in a new liturgical revival. Heinrich Hansen published his *Stimuli et clavi,* a new series of ninety-five Theses, in 1917. Under the leadership of Friedrich Heiler, ably seconded by Adolf Glinz, Oscar Mehl, Karl Ramge, Paul Schorlemmer, and others, an articulate and scholarly liturgical movement challenged the prevailing apathy with its fourfold emphasis on evangelical justification by faith, the gospel of *sola gratia,* Pauline freedom from the Law, and the alleged primitive primacy of the prophetic-pneumatic charisma over the official-hierarchical element in the Church.

Nor were they alone. The Berneuchen circle of 1923— which created an organ for itself in the Confraternity of St. Michael (Michaelsbruderschaft) in 1931—has endeavored under the inspiration of Dr. (later Landesbischof) Wilhelm Staehlin, aided by Karl Berhard Ritter, Walter Lotz, Ernst Jansen, H. D. Wendland, Christhard Mahrenholz, Horst Schumann, and others, to furnish a theological basis for a liturgical revival that would encompass the entire German Evangelical Church.

The Alpirsbacher Work, begun in 1933, currently under the leadership of Friedrich Buchholz, has sought to find in the objectivity of Gregorian a symbol of that unity of the Church which transcends time and cultures. In the 'thirties Paul Graff, through his monumental *Geschichte der Aufloesung der alten Gottesdienstlichen Formen in der evangelische Kirche Deutschlands,* taught the world what it had lost. The neo-Lutheranism of the Erlangen Theological Faculty— men like Herman Sasse, Paul Althaus, Ernst Sommerlath—had liturgical repercussions.

The Nazi attack upon the Church restricted the liturgical movement's expression but it could not eradicate the liturgical impulse. If anything, many parts of the Confessing Church in Germany lived by and from the liturgy, so that the Hitlerian persecution gave a new stimulus to liturgical life.

The wartime and post-World War II contributions of Hans Asmussen, Peter Brunner, Karl Ferdinand Müller, and Eduard Schlink have added their names to the roster of distinguished contributors to the liturgical revival. Notable developments in Germany include a pan-Lutheran hymnal and service book, the publication of the five-volume liturgical magnum opus, *Leiturgia* (of which about three-quarters is in print), and the international *Jahrbuch für Liturgik und Hymnologie,* now in process of publication, beginning with Volume I in 1955.

The between-the-wars German liturgical movement had its counterpart in Scandinavia, in such groups as the Danish Brotherhood of St. Ansgar and the Pro Ecclesia Union in Norway. In Sweden, the liturgical movement embraced a wide continuum of emphases, from the Romanizing of Kåre Skredsvik through the pro-Anglican neo-scholasticism of Gunnar Rosendal, to the more normally Lutheran work of men like Artur Adell, Knut Peters, Bishop Bo Harald Giertz, Pehr Edwall, Bishop Yngve Brilioth, Bengt Strömberg, Sven Kjöllerström, and Albert Lysander.

The European Lutheran liturgical movement supplied some stimuli to the Lutheran liturgical movement on this continent, and there has been a limited exchange of personnel and material; but the Lutheran liturgical revival in America is a thoroughly indigenous movement, evoked by American rather than by European theological and ecclesiastical developments. Only so can it be understood.

The liturgical movement can probably best be studied in

the literature which it has produced during the past three decades. This literature exists largely in the form of articles in periodicals, like the *American Lutheran, Lutheran Church Art, The Church Builder, Pro Ecclesia Lutherana, Sursum Corda, Una Sancta,* Edgar S. Brown's column in *The Lutheran,* and the *Proceedings of the Liturgical Institute* of Valparaiso University, the bulletins of various liturgical societies, a few monographs, and a number of tracts. A comprehensive history remains to be compiled.

One line of descent goes back to the Confessional revival in older American Lutheranism, which created the Common Service of the Lutheran Church in 1888. A link is furnished by the Lutheran Liturgical Association, which flourished at the beginning of this century, and the seven volumes of whose *Memoirs* still furnish a vast treasury of liturgical learning. From the Common Service Book of 1888 can be traced the lines that run down to the 1941 Synodical Conference Service Book and to the 1958 Intersynodical Service Book.

The Lutheran liturgical movement is frequently equated with and condemned as preoccupation with aestheticism, ritualism, or ceremonialism. It would be inaccurate to deny an interest in these things on the part of almost everyone associated with the liturgical movement, but a preoccupation with any or all of these points mentioned would not be characteristic of a serious liturgical concern. Failure to discuss the artistic and cultural impact of the liturgical movement in this discussion, however, must not be interpreted as a depreciation of this important aspect of church life. But I should like, in any case, to chronicle the recent organization of the Lutheran Society for Worship, Music and the Arts. The chief concern of the Lutheran liturgical movement has been and is a theological and a practical one.

I repeat that the liturgical movement in the Lutheran Church on this continent is an indigenous one, evoked by American rather than by European conditions. Compared to the Church in Europe, the Lutheran Church in America has for the past century been on the whole consistently more Biblical, more Catholic, more Lutheran, and more Orthodox, in the sixteenth- and seventeenth-century sense. The Bible may not have been studied as zealously as it might have been, either by our pastors or by our people, but its truthfulness has not been denounced from our pulpits. The Symbolical Books may have been neglected, but they have never been repudiated. And while Lutheran synods and Lutheran theologians have differed from one another, what kept us apart was generally our zeal for our respective orthodoxies rather than the European indifference that would tolerate even sub-Nicene theology if it were presented in a scholarly enough fashion. This background is an integral part of the Lutheran liturgical movement.

In defining specific theological and practical emphases which are particularly characteristic of the movement, it is impossible to generalize with complete accuracy. The liturgical movement is a movement, not an organization. Each representative has his own characteristic complex or syndrome of emphases. In what follows, I am trying to indicate these points on which there would be fairly consistent agreement, but I do not wish to suggest that every articulate representative of the movement has expressed them or would agree to these specific formulations.

In general, while their common liturgical concern and interest create a genuine bond that transcends synodical lines, liturgically minded Lutherans tend to conform to whatever synodical pattern exists. Thus the Scandinavians tend to reveal the warm-hearted piety that has become a part of their tradition, the United Lutheran churchmen the generous tolerance that they have learned in the unification process which their body has undergone, and the Missourians their characteristic conservatism and confidence in the processes of education.

The Lutheran liturgical movement is not strongly institutionalized. There are many small groups that meet for prayer and study, but no national organization has proved viable. Probably the largest group at present is the two-year-old Fellowship of St. Augustine, with roughly two hundred members, who pray God to raise up in the Church of the Augsburg Confession on this continent men and women to serve Him and the Church in evangelical communities. The organ of the movement is the quarterly, *Una Sancta,* privately published. Opportunities for personal contact of supporters of the movement are provided by the annual sessions of the Institute for Liturgical Studies of Valparaiso University, sometimes held on the school's Indiana campus, sometimes elsewhere.

A common characteristic of the Lutheran liturgical movement is a cordial lack of enthusiasm for Roman Catholicism. The efforts of liturgically minded Roman Catholics at recovering an evangelical Christianity are regarded with sympathy; usable results of Roman Catholic scholarly research are received with gratitude; and friendly interpersonal relations with individual liturgically minded Roman Catholics are carefully cultivated. At the same time, opponents of the liturgical movement have so often and so violently accused the movement's proponents of popery and Romanizing, and overzealous Roman Catholics have so often misrepresented the Lutheran movement as a surrender of Lutheran principle in favor of Roman Catholic claims, that representatives of the Lutheran liturgical movement have developed a kind of anti-Roman sensitization.

In the process of restoring rites and ceremonies, there is a tendency, wherever an option exists, to choose the form which differs from, rather than that which conforms to, Roman Catholic practice. The fact that many sixteenth-century Lutheran usages preserve older forms than the corresponding Roman Catholic developments is much stressed. Thus in chasubles, the Latin fiddle-back model is generally rejected in favor of the fuller Gothic type, which careful and conservative Roman Catholic canonists regard as liturgically unlawful in the Latin rite. In making the sign of the holy Cross, the earlier form, in which the last movement is from the right to the left rather than from the left to the right, as in the Latin rite, is often urged. It is pointed out that having two candles on the altar is better supported in Lutheran tradition than the post-Reformation Roman norm of six. This list might be extended to considerable length. At the same time, where lapsed and lapsing Roman Catholics constitute a large part of a Lutheran parish's missionary potential, liturgically minded Lutheran pastors have, in the interest of a more effective evangelistic outreach, on occasion conformed on some points as far as they conscientiously could to Roman Catholic procedure, such as wearing Latin-type birettas and cassocks and lace-trimmed albs and surplices, or conducting Tre Ore services on Good Friday.

Toward Eastern Orthodoxy the attitude of protagonists of the Lutheran liturgical movement has been, up till now at least, quite cordial, although the informal contacts have been limited almost wholly to communities with considerable constituencies in both communions.

With reference to the Protestant Episcopal Church, the attitude is less consistent. Particularly those who stand in the tradition of the creators of the Common Service and the Lutheran Liturgical Association exhibit a strong receptiveness to Anglican influence. This is understandable. In the eastern United States, the tradition of friendly co-operation with the Protestant Episcopal Church is a long one. In the early part of this century almost the only usable scholarly liturgiological studies in English were by Anglicans. The compilers of the Common Service Book had defended their extensive borrowings of formulations from the Book of Common Prayer by pointing out that the edition of 1549 was essentially a Lutheran rite in English; yet the substantial verbatim identity of extensive sections of the Common Service Book and the Book of Common Prayer had a subtle effect on the users of the former. At many points, the late medieval uses of the Church of England agreed with the contemporary uses of the Continental dioceses and provinces that became Lutheran in the Reformation, in contrast to the changing Roman use that was gradually invading Northern Europe. The Protestant Episcopal Church in the East was long the bearer of what was aesthetically and unquestionably the best American tradition of church architecture and church music.

The influence of the Protestant Episcopal Church upon the Lutheran liturgical movement has been both formal and substantial. An example of formal influence is the widespread adoption in Lutheran circles of the nineteenth-century Anglican surplice-and-stole combination, for which there is no historic Lutheran precedent. An example of a substantial influence is the position of the Invocation of the Holy Ghost after the Words of Institution in the Eucharistic Prayer of the new *Service Book and Hymnal* prepared by the Intersynodical Commission on the Liturgy, a position that reflects the theory of consecration through the Epiclesis, in contrast to the Western doctrine, shared by the Lutheran Confessions, of consecration through the Words of Institution.

It must be admitted, however, that some other representatives of the Lutheran liturgical movement, notably in the Middle West, tend here and there to be anti-Anglican more or less on principle. The motivation in these cases is likely to be complex and not wholly theological.

Over against the Protestant denominations, representatives of the Lutheran liturgical movement tend to emphasize the Catholicity of Lutheran doctrine and practice. Sometimes the emphasis on Lutheran ceremonial is designed as a prophylactic against lapsing into Protestantism; as a denominational pedagogical device; as a witness to the historic continuity of the Lutheran Church with its Catholic past; as a protest against the view that the Lutheran Church is merely an emphasis in Protestantism; and as a disavowal of the misconception that Lutheran theology is merely 'fundamentalism' plus baptismal regeneration and some kind of doctrine of the Real Presence.

The liturgical movement in the Lutheran Church is strongly confessional. It insists that Lutheran pastors and Lutheran parishes must take the Symbolical Books seriously, in the belief that such a serious acceptance of the Confessions will inevitably carry with it acceptance of the major theses of the liturgical revival: the importance of evangelical preaching and intensive Biblical study; the necessity of the sacraments for the Church and for the individual Christian; the significance of Baptism as participation in the death and resurrection of our Lord; the recognition of the need for individual Absolution and of the desirability of private Confession; the restoration of the Holy Eucharist to its historic place as the chief parochial service of the congregation; a due appreciation of the role of the sacred Ministry; and the value of fraternal admonition and counsel by all Christians.

Because the early efforts of the liturgical movement were challenged with the accusation that they were un-Lutheran innovations, there has been an increasingly strong cultivation of a historical sense and a diligent examination of the pre-Pietistic literary monuments of the Lutheran religion as a prophylactic against unwarranted innovations that militate against the essential spirit of the conservative Reformation of the sixteenth century.

To the liturgically minded Lutheran the sacred Scriptures are an absolute norm and the only source of doctrine. The Symbolical Books of the Lutheran Church—that is, the three Catholic Creeds, the Augsburg Confession (1530) and its Apology (1531), the Smalcald Articles (1537) and the Tractatus on the Authority and Primacy of the Pope (1537), the two Catechisms (1528–29) and the Formula of Concord with its own Preface (1577–80)—participate in this normative authority of the sacred Scriptures. They stand as a demonstration of the essential Catholicity of the Lutheran Church, and constitute a necessary standard of doctrine and practice for those who profess to be Lutheran. Any supplementary statement of doctrine, ancient, sixteenth-century, or recent, private or corporate, is only a witness to the conviction of those who promulgated or subscribed it. From this it will appear that the theological differences between liturgically minded Lutherans and those who profess no sympathy with the liturgical movement are likely to be differences of emphasis.

In contrast to the tendency to overintellectualize faith and to make the ministry consist almost exclusively in preaching and teaching, the liturgical movement emphasizes the practical recovery of all the evangelical means of grace, in the spirit of Article IV of Part III of the Smalcald Articles, which sees as forms of the gospel the proclaimed Word, Holy Baptism, the sacrament of the altar, the office of the keys, and the mutual conversation and consolation of Christians.

In its doctrine of the Church, the liturgical movement interprets the phrases of the Catholic Creeds as they were originally intended, insofar as that intention is recoverable and relevant. It follows the Symbolical Books both in avoiding the visible-invisible antithesis and in stressing on the one hand the empirical and this-worldly aspect of the Church as an institution for the salvation of its members, and on the other hand the Church as a corporate community and association of believers whose faith is nourished by the means of grace.

On Church polity, the liturgical movement holds that as long as the sacred Ministry is maintained in the Church, matters of constitution and polity are adiaphora. At the same time, it shares with the Apology of the Augsburg Confession the conviction that restoration of the historic episcopate is a desideratum. Realistically it does not regard such a development as likely to be realized in the Lutheran Church of this country at an early date. While it thus regards the historic episcopate as an invaluable symbol of Catholic continuity, comparable to the Catholic formulations of the faith and the Catholic ceremonial and ritual which it has retained, it explicitly holds that the episcopate is at most part of the *bene esse* of the Church and by no means necessary either to the essence of the Church or to the validity of the sacraments which Lutheran priests administer.

With the Symbolical Books, it teaches the necessity of the sacraments, stresses their primary dynamic significance as actions rather than things, and emphasizes co-ordination of the *verbum visibile* and the *sacramentum audibile*. It holds that the definition, and the number, of the sacraments is relatively immaterial. (It should be observed that in primitive Lutheran theology 'sacrament' is not an a priori genus, of which the individual sacraments are species, but that 'sacrament' is an a posteriori synthetic concept inductively arrived at.) With the Symbols, the Lutheran liturgical movement explicitly identifies as sacraments Holy Baptism, Holy Absolution, and the Holy Eucharist, and concedes the term to Holy Orders and Holy Matrimony. It insists that Lutheran theology is both Trinity-centered and Christ-centered, both Incarnation-centered and Atonement-centered, and that its sacramental orientation is a fundamental consequence of this centrality of the Atonement wrought by the incarnate Word of God.

Since Holy Baptism is essential, the liturgical movement urges that this sacrament be administered as soon as possible after the birth of a child. In accordance with historic Lutheran practice, it discountenances 'sprinkling' as the term is usually understood among Protestants, and urges, as a minimum, Baptism by trine affusion of water in such quantity that it runs.

The liturgical movement places great emphasis upon the frequent celebration and reception of Holy Communion. It holds that our Lord did not intend that the Blessed Sacrament be bound to specific times, but that it be available to His people whenever they gather together for worship. It urges therefore that our parishes restore the old Lutheran custom of celebrating the Blessed Sacrament at the main parochial service or services every Sunday and major holy day, and of making it available frequently in addition as the devotion of the people requires.

The liturgical movement rejects transubstantiation, as defined by our separated Latin brethren. While it concedes that it is proper to speak of the presence of the living Christ in the

Blessed Sacrament, it insists that an adequate doctrine must also expressly affirm the real and essential presence of Christ's Body and Blood in the Holy Eucharist, in the spirit of the statement of the Smalcald Articles: 'In the Holy Communion the bread and wine are the Body and Blood of Christ.' It rejects artolatry, but urges with the Formula of Concord that only an Arian heretic would refuse to adore the Son of God present in the sacramental action.

On the question of reservation for the Communion of the sick, there is a difference of opinion. Some hold it to be wrong; others hold it to be tolerable, but undesirable; others reserve in both kinds.

With the Large Catechism, the liturgical movement recommends the rule of St. Hilary of Poitiers, that eligible communicants should receive at every celebration unless they have committed a sin for which, if it were publicly known, they could be excommunicated.

With reference to Holy Absolution, the liturgical movement echoes the repeated declarations of the Symbolical Books in favor of the retention of individual absolution. While conceding the validity of Holy Absolution when pronounced over a number of penitents at one time, it regards such a procedure as contrary to the historic practice of the Lutheran Church and to the spirit of the sacrament.

It regards the restoration of individual absolution (which can follow a general confession) and the restoration of private confession as two separate issues, although it urges the restoration also of the latter as an important aspect of an adequate pastoral ministry.

While stressing the Scriptural doctrine of the universal priesthood of the baptized, the liturgical movement holds with Article V of the Augsburg Confession that the sacred Ministry is the divinely appointed agency for the imparting of justifying faith through the gospel and the sacraments.

The liturgical movement stresses the readiness of the Symbolical Books to concede sacramental status to both the sacred Ministry and the rite of Holy Ordination by the laying-on of hands, and their deliberate indorsement of the conception of the twofold authority of order and jurisdiction. With the Symbolical Books it holds that the sacred Ministry is an order as well as an office. And it stresses the doctrine of the Tractate Concerning Authority and Primacy of the Pope that when a pastor in his own church administers Holy Ordination to a fit candidate this is by divine right (*jure divino*) unquestionably effective and rightful.

As a safeguard of the doctrine of the complete humanity of our Lord, which the fundamentalism of our times relegates into the background, the liturgical movement stresses the evangelical Mariology of the Symbolical Books, which call her ever-virgin, most holy, that most praiseworthy Virgin, the Mother of God, and most deserving of the amplest honors; which declare that she bore our Lord without violation of her virginity; and which concede that she, like the other saints in light, prays for the Church in general.

The liturgical movement takes seriously the unity in Christ of the faithful departed with the members of the Church militant here in earth, and reminds the Church that the Symbolical Books explicitly state that they do not forbid prayers for the faithful departed, and that they do not endorse the opinion that prayers for the faithful departed are useless.

It affirms that New Testament worship is essentially faith and the fruits of faith, and that external ceremonies ordained by men are not in themselves worship or any part of worship. But the liturgical movement also affirms the double-rhythmed sacrificial-sacramental character of all worship, and insists, with Article XXIV of the Apology of the Augsburg Confession, that the Mass can properly be spoken of as a Eucharistic sacrifice.

Thus, conscious of the Catholicity of the Lutheran position, the Lutheran liturgical movement seriously seeks the fullest implementation of that position in the Church's liturgical life and practice, in the conviction that the recovery of this practical expression of its Catholicity is a necessary prerequisite to the Lutheran Church's full contribution to the ecumenical conversation of Christendom.

IV

THE SOCIAL IMPLICATIONS OF THE
LITURGICAL RENEWAL

The Right Reverend Arthur Carl Lichtenberger,
D.D., S.T.D.

*Presiding Bishop of the
Protestant Episcopal Church,
Sometime Bishop of Missouri*

THE SOCIAL IMPLICATIONS OF THE
LITURGICAL RENEWAL

ACCORDING to the Shorter Oxford Dictionary, the word 'imply' means to enfold, enwrap, entangle, involve, or comprise logically. I take it that the word 'implication' in the title of this address carries that meaning. When we consider the social implications of the liturgical renewal we are not concerned with something peripheral but with the heart of the matter. The liturgical renewal necessarily enfolds, enwraps, and involves social witness and social action. Father Louis Bouyer has written:

Perhaps the greatest, and certainly the most difficult problem for liturgical piety is the one which awaits us when we go out of the church after the liturgical celebration is finished. For, if there is any one point that our study has brought out, it is that the importance of the liturgical celebration itself implies a correlative importance in what we do, after the liturgical celebration, in daily living.[1]

The scene of that daily living is the world where no one can live to himself, and where the distinction between a personal gospel and a social gospel has no meaning. The gospel is one and bears upon all human life; collective as well as individual actions stand under the judgment of God. What we do together is of no less concern to God than what we do separ-

1 *Liturgical Piety* (University of Notre Dame Press, 1955), p. 257.

ately. As our hearts are open to God, our desires known, so the ordering of our common life is known to Him for He is acquainted with all our ways.

The social implications of the liturgical renewal, then, arise out of the gospel itself and can be seen in many of the basic convictions which gave rise to the revival and which inform it.

To begin with, there is that basic conviction in which it is rooted and grounded, that worship is at the heart and center of a Christian's life. Worship is not a means to a better life for me or a better social order for us all; worship is an end in itself. The ordering and conduct of worship is the one distinctive and essential task of the Church. Dean Sperry in *Reality in Worship*, one of the very early books on the liturgical revival written in this country, says:

In the large sense of the word, therefore, the ordering and conduct of public worship is the distinctive task of the church . . . In seeming to do nothing for the world it does all for the world, or at least does that without which no human effort can ever be made perfect. The other ministries of the church are all peripheral, incidental, derivative, and with perfect propriety may be shared with other institutions or relinquished to them. This is central and inalienable.

So long as the church bids men to the worship of God and provides a simple and credible vehicle for worship it need not question its place, mission, and influence in the world. If it loses faith in the act of worship, is thoughtless in the ordering of worship, and careless in the conduct of worship, it need not look to its avocations to save it. It is dead at its heart, and no chafing of the extremities, producing what Carlyle called 'quaint galvanic sprawlings,' will bring back the life that has left it.[2]

[2] Willard L. Sperry, *Reality in Worship* (Macmillan, 1926), p. 168.

We do not worship God in order that we may receive certain personal benefits; we do not worship God in order that we may have peace and justice among men and nations. We worship God and give thanks to Him for all the benefits we receive at His hands; we worship Him and pray that we may be strengthened to do His will; we worship Him and offer ourselves as instruments of His justice and peace. This is the order, and the order here is of first importance. First, 'Our Father who art in heaven, Hallowed be thy Name'; then, 'Thy kingdom come, thy will be done.' If we are to obey His will and work for the kingdom, we must first of all hallow the Name.

Unfortunately, a man may worship and yet be turned inward upon himself, a parish may become parochial, a Church a sect. This, of course, is not the product of Christian worship itself, but is the result of a particular view of the relationship of God to His creation and, following from that, the perceived purpose of worship. This, in general, is the subjective view of Christianity in which the emphasis is largely upon personal piety and individual personal morality, and where a sharp line of distinction is drawn between the natural and the supernatural, the secular and the sacred.

One manifestation of this subjectivism is the Pietist movement that was so strong in Germany as early as the seventeenth century and is still strong today. Pietism no doubt saved the Protestant Churches in Germany and other parts of Europe from a sterile orthodoxy. But in the end, the Church became separated from the world, fragmentized into small groups of believers. By now they use language which only they can understand; their faith brings them rich personal blessings, but they are content not only to let the world (in every sense) go by, but believe on principle that they should. There is little recognition that, in Bonhoeffer's phrase, 'God wants to be praised in the midst of the world.'

However, such subjectivism is no more characteristic of Protestant and Evangelical than of Catholic Churches. There is ample evidence of its existence in the Middle Ages, and it is still a strong element in contemporary Roman Catholic piety. Abbé Michonneau has given us a classic description of this in what he calls a typical scene in church:

> The Low Mass is going on. A few men are standing up at the back of the church and gazing around. Further up, the church is pretty well filled, with women mostly; some are saying their beads, to the accompaniment of clicking and audible 'Hail Marys.' Some are reading prayer books or missals. Some are seated while the rest kneel; for no apparent reason there are periodic reverses of position. Only during the reading of the Gospel is the whole church in the same position. . . . Obviously (the priest) is isolated, cut off from the people behind him. Obviously the people in that church are not a community, but a mere collection of individuals, praying individually as best they can.[3]

It would be very difficult to discover the social implications of such worship. No doubt there are individual benefits, but if this is the nature of liturgical action, then when one leaves the service he leaves as an isolated individual, not as a member of a fellowship, of a body which has a mission in the world. It is, as we know, partly as a corrective to such individualism and subjectivism that the liturgical revival emphasizes the corporate nature of Christian worship and the importance of liturgical patterns and structures.

Here then is another relevant principle emphasized by the Liturgical Movement: Christian worship is essentially cor-

[3] *Revolution in a City Parish* (Newman Press, 1949), p. 26.

porate. The worship by which the Church is fed, the worship which is its distinctive task, has a particular character, and, broadly speaking, a given pattern. A congregation at worship is not 'a collection of individuals praying individually as best they can'; a congregation is a community, a corporate body.

It is not precisely true to say, however, as I just did, that Christian worship is essentially corporate. For it is both personal and corporate. When I go to church, I confess my own sins, I profess my belief, I make my own personal commitment, I offer my own praise and thanksgiving. I receive the bread and wine as the Body and Blood of our Lord which was given for me. As J. S. Whale has said, 'Religion is always inescapably personal. Religion without this would be like love without any lovers to illustrate it.' This is true surely of the Christian religion. But the worship which I offer as an individual is not offered privately. My own personal acts of worship are set in the pattern of liturgical action which is the action of the Church, the assembly of God.

Robinson Crusoe, it has been remarked, could not be a Christian until he found his man Friday. However that might be, it is certainly true that to be reconciled to God through Christ is to be brought into a relationship with others in the household of faith. This is evident in Baptism. The child is given his name which is his alone; he is received, we believe, by God as his own child. At the same time, he is received into the congregation of Christ's flock. His sponsors are there as representatives of the parish, and the members of the congregation take on the responsibilities of the family of God to do their part that the child may lead the rest of his life according to this beginning. He is baptized into the Church, which is prior to him not only in time but in essence.

This means, furthermore, that he is baptized into the mission of the Church. This is the baptism with which Christ was baptized; this is our baptism. It is the sacrament of individual salvation, surely, but through Baptism we are made members of Christ to pray and work and suffer that all men in their corporate life may be reconciled to God, that our culture and society may be baptized into Christ.

All this is largely obscured when children or adults are baptized privately after a morning or an evening service when most of the congregation has gone home, or when Baptism is administered at some odd hour with only the parents and relatives and a few friends present. This is a most effective way of by-passing the social implications of Baptism. Baptism, and therefore Church membership, is made to appear as a private affair, essentially; the center of the action is the child and his own family in their relationship to God, not the child and his incorporation into the Church as God's child. Fortunately, however, Baptism now is generally administered publicly. This is one of the most evident fruits of the liturgical revival in our own Church—this and the more thorough preparation of parents and sponsors. The effects of this will be considerable in time. There will be a deeper understanding of both the personal and corporate nature of Church membership and of the function of the Church in society.

When in Baptism we have been made members of Christ, what we do is no longer simply our own business. We are members one of another. Our actions affect the other members of the fellowship, their actions affect us. We are responsible as individuals and we act through constant choices as persons, but as persons who are part of an organic whole. In all we do we represent the Church, and in all we do we are supported by the fact that we are members of a concerned group. Our actions are held together by the corporate life of the congregation. Christian worship by its very nature proclaims this.

Actually, of course, we do not find much evidence of this relationship, of corporate action and social responsibility. But I am not at the moment describing how we live together as Church, but rather the kind of life to which we are called. When we do see the Church living this way, we recognize it as the real thing.

Bishop Newbigin in *A South India Diary* tells the story of a group of newly baptized Christians who were boycotted by their Hindu landlords. The converts were from the lowest social stratum, and the Hindus were bitter about their conversion and did all they could to make them suffer for it. They would not allow the Christians to use the wells; other workers were imported from another village to take over the work formerly done by the Christians. Every sort of pressure was used to force them to renounce their faith, but the Christians all stood together against this. Then, as Bishop Newbigin says,

. . . there was a very serious weakening. Fourteen of the Christian men, driven to dull despair by hunger and unemployment, decided to submit. 'What is the good of it! What's the good of all this misery for the sake of a little bit of ash.' [If they smeared their foreheads with the sacred ash of Siva all would be well.] 'Come on, we'll go and put it on.' They went in a body to the Hindu temple, telling the priest of their intention. Two crowds were watching. On one side, between the temple and the outcaste quarter, the Christians who had learned of the defection stood at a distance and watched. On the other side, stood the Hindus . . . There was a moment of silence, while [the Christians] stood on the very brink of apostasy. Then one after another spoke: 'Do what you will; we cannot do this.' Together they turned and walked back towards their fellow Christians.[4]

[4] J. E. Lesslie Newbigin, *A South India Diary* (SCM Press Ltd., 1951), pp. 89–90.

What the final outcome of this episode was, I do not know. The action of these Christians did bring an end to attempts in other villages to bring the same sort of pressure on other Christians, and there were no more near capitulations to the Hindus. All over that part of the Church of South India the Christians held together. Their bishops and other leaders did what they could to help. And all this taken together, as Bishop Newbigin said, 'this is what has frightened the caste people because this must in the end mean revolution.'

Such a predicament is quite outside our experience, but what these Indian Christians did in their circumstances we can do in ours. Facing persecution and starvation, they stood against a common enemy and they knew that common action was needed—common action, but each man making his own decision in the strength of his own faith, upheld and supported by the Church. This is the Church taking action in the social order, the Church in which, as Gregory the Great said, 'each one supports the other and in turn is supported by the other.' This is the Church taking action through its members who have a sense of their common salvation and interrelatedness in Christ. The Church cannot provide ready-made solutions to economic and political problems, either by official pronouncements or in any other way. Those who call upon the Church to act in one situation or another seem to expect something of this sort, evidently. But the Church as an institution is, I believe, incapable of saying either Yes or No to many of the major political and social questions of the day, which means that the Church is not equal to the historical events of our time. This, however, does not relieve us as individuals of our responsibility for decision and action. The social witness of the Church is relevant and effective when that witness is made by its members in their corporate life.

As the font stands at the entrance to the church, so the

altar is at its center. As in Baptism we are incorporated into the Church, enlisted under Christ's banner so that we may confess Him, fight against injustice and oppression, and witness for Him by our lives in the midst of the world, so in the Eucharist we are given both food and pattern for the life to which we are committed. When plans for the new cathedral in Coventry were first projected, the instructions to the architects were: design the altar and then build the church around it. From much evidence still before us in brick and stone, there was a time in this country when architects designed the nave and chancel, then added a sanctuary where, in the smallest possible space, high and lifted up, an altar was placed against the east wall. This is the architectural heritage of many congregations, but even where this is the setting of worship, it can be made quite evident that the altar is a family table around which the people gather, and that the distinctive Christian act of worship is the Eucharist. And as it is the distinctive act of the Church, so the Eucharist is at the center of the Christian's life; all his life is touched and shaped by it.

As Church, we are not indifferent to the world, we are not set over against the world in hostility to it; our salvation is bound up with the salvation of the whole created order. We are not to be saved apart from the world (cosmos) but with it. This is the vision of the Old Testament prophets; this is the expectation written in the New Testament. Man and social order, man and created nature, are to be transformed, made into that image in the likeness of which they were created and which we see dimly now. Man is not isolated from the rest of creation. This is what St. Paul is saying in the Epistle to the Romans (8:20–21):

The world of creation cannot as yet see Reality, not because it chooses to be blind, but because in God's purpose it has been so limited—yet it has been given hope. And the hope is that in the end the whole of created life will be rescued from the tyranny of change and decay, and have its share in that magnificent liberty which can only belong to the children of God! (J. B. Phillips' translation.)

This is the hope which is before us each time we do the Eucharist; this is the way the Church lives, having salvation as a present possession and yet hoping for it. We are to pray and work that God's will may be done on earth. In the liturgy of the Church of South India, after the recitation of the words of institution, the people respond: 'Amen. Thy death, O Lord, we commemorate, thy resurrection we confess, and thy second coming we await.'

As we await the second coming of the Lord, as we proclaim the Lord's death till He come, we do not live in a world of worship and piety apart from the world we encounter at home, in office, or factory, or on the street. In the Eucharist we are made aware that our lives are lived on the boundary, the frontier between the Kingdom and this present world of sin, suffering, and death, and that at every point we are met by Christ whose grace is offered not as a means of escape from the world but as power to transform us and all life. While we were yet sinners, while we were yet in this untransformed world, we were brought into the restored order of God's kingdom through Baptism. We have been made citizens of His Kingdom. This is proclaimed each time we celebrate the liturgy; here is the word of God in law and prophecy, in promise and demand. This is the gospel which tells us who we are and why we are here. This is the gospel which comes to us as a deed done.

> Glorious, most glorious is the crown
> Of him that brought salvation down

By meekness, called man's son;
Seers that stupendous truth believed,
And now the matchless deed's achieved,
Determined, dared, and done.

Confronted with this gospel, we are made to choose. If we draw near with faith, we are offering ourselves to God to be transformed and used by Him in this world. The kingdom is in this act, at least, realized. And the implication is clear: we are sent out from the church to live in the world the life that has been lived and received in the Eucharist. Is a man to live that life when he is in his home but not when he is at his business? Is it an operative force for relations with a friend but not with an employee? Is such life practicable and possible for an individual, but not for a number of individuals acting as a group? To ask such questions, it seems to me, is to answer them. There was a time, you remember, when a man could say, 'Things have come to a pretty pass when religion is allowed to interfere with a man's private life.' It is no less absurd to say, 'Things have come to a pretty pass when Christianity is allowed to interfere with a man's social or political or economic life.' The gospel speaks to the totality of life. All that we do, individually or together, stands under the judgment of God, and all our ways are to be conformed to His will.

There is one more point, emphasized by the Liturgical Movement, which has particular relevance to this subject. It is the revival of lay participation in worship and the breaking down of the walls of partition between the ordained ministry and the laity. It is curious that one effect of the Oxford Movement was to strengthen, on the whole, the wall of partition between priest and people. Thomas Arnold said that, while the disciples of the Oxford Movement were rightly concerned with recovering a high doctrine of the Church, what they produced was a high doctrine of the ministry. 'The effect of this was to make a separation between clergy and laity, ascribing to the former what belonged to the whole Body and making the life of the Church dependent on its ordained ministry. Thus, in a sense, ordination had been made more important than baptism.'[5] When this happens the true meaning of liturgy is obscured, and as a result the distinction between sacred and secular is hardened into an absolute distinction.

The liturgical revival, in contrast to this, insists that liturgical action is the action of the Church, that every member of the Body has his liturgy to offer. There are no spectators at the Eucharist; the action is not done by a few for the edification of the many. Do you know the story of the catechumen who asked the priest, 'What is the position of the layman in the Catholic Church?' The priest answered, 'There are two positions of the layman in the Catholic Church, kneeling at Mass and sitting when the priest is in the pulpit.' Cardinal Gasquet, who told this story, said he should have added a third: 'hand in pocketbook.' As the people share in worship— in both word and sacrament, for preaching is an act of the Church and to be effective must find a response in the listeners—so the worship of the people is an offering to God of the wholeness of community life. The people offer to God in penitence and in praise all that each individual has been doing all week, the common life in which their work and leisure has been set; and the people through the offering of this sacrifice, in union with the perfect sacrifice of Christ and through communion with Him, are sent out into the world to serve Him there.

[5] Denis Payne, 'Christianizing the Nation and Edifying the Church,' *Theology* LIX (February 1956), p. 61.

These, then, are some of the social implications of the liturgical renewal. But are the people in parishes that have been strongly influenced by the movement aware of them and concerned about them, so that they are struggling with the difficult and complex problems involved in Christian social witness and action? I do not know; but I do know that vast numbers of Church people are quite ignorant of these implications.

For example, a study of four parishes in the Diocese of Birmingham has been published under the title *The Church's Understanding of Itself*. In the chapter on 'The Fellowship of the Congregation,' there is this observation: 'With the exception of the nuclear members of each congregation they [i.e. the congregations] were collections of individuals who met together to worship as they would on other social occasions.' It was quite evident from the expressed opinion of members of these congregations that the majority of people were unaware of any actual tension between the values of the Church and the values of society. In one parish, most members were more conscious of the difference between the Catholic and Protestant distinctions of the Anglican Church than they were of any distinction between the Church and the world. In only one parish out of four was there a considerable group of people who understood the Church as a fellowship through which God would leaven and redeem the world. In the other three, the generally held view of the Church was that it is a kind of club brought into existence by church-going, an agency for the teaching of sound morals.

But it is unnecessary to look to England for evidence of this sort. We have it on every hand in our own Church; we cannot help but see it. Twenty-three years ago, Father Hebert wrote in *Liturgy and Society*: 'We have not only to consider what to do with Christ in the Church, but what He wills to do with us in the street. The Church has indeed the key of the street. Too often she seems inclined to use it to lock herself in.'[6] We have not changed. In the Episcopal Church, we are particularly careful of our treasure. We not only guard it closely, we are inclined to embroider the napkin in which we lay away our talent.

But there are disturbers of our peace. The liturgical revival, the renewed interest in Biblical theology, the Ecumenical Movement, have produced a ferment which is at work. It does not show itself at present in noticeable action; if we look for much visible evidence of the Church's social witness, we shall not find it. The Church must once again hear the gospel and learn how it speaks to all life before the Church can act. But—and this is the necessary thing if the Church is to be relevant to life—there is an increasing awareness of the tension between the Church at worship and the community at work. When we see in the liturgy the pattern of the restored order of God's kingdom, then the contrast between that order and our own personal and social life is very evident and very great. If we are not aware of that tension, then the Church is in peril. The Church is not irrelevant because of its present failure to bear strong witness in social action; it is irrelevant when we do not feel the tension between liturgy and life.

There is a further point here. We are more likely to be aware of the contrast between the pattern of life set before us in the liturgy and the structure and organization of our economic and political and social life than we are of the contrast between the pattern of the liturgy and the way we live together as Church in our local congregations. Liturgy

[6] A. G. Hebert, *Liturgy and Society* (Faber and Faber, 1935), p. 182.

and Church seem to be of one piece, liturgy and the world
set sharply over against each other. It is hard to believe that
anyone could live in a parish as layman or clergyman very
long and not be disabused of that notion, but we do easily
deceive ourselves. So instead of turning to the world at work,
let us look at the Church in one aspect of its own life for an
example of an area in which the Church is called to bear
witness and to act. This does not mean that the Church as an
institution can be isolated from the cultural patterns of the
nation and the age. The way we live in the world is reflected,
of course, in the way we live in the Church. But now we are
examining one characteristic of the Church's own life.

The Church—I speak now of the Episcopal Church—in
contrast to the order of life which we live out in the liturgy,
is quite clearly a segregated society. I refer not to the segregation of races but the segregation of sexes. The pattern
of organization, of the functioning of the Church, is that of
an age-old masculine pattern. Women are not generally allowed to share fully with men in a complementary relationship. It is only in recent years and in some dioceses that
women have been allowed by canon to serve on vestries or sit
as delegates in diocesan conventions. All attempts to have
women accepted in the male precincts of the House of Deputies have been valiantly turned aside. Whatever place women
have been given in the governing bodies of the Church has
been through haphazard, if determined, efforts. We have
been greatly concerned with men and women in the marriage
relationship, but hardly at all with men and women as persons working together in the Church or the world. The World
Council of Churches has a Department on the Co-operation
of Men and Women in Church and Society which has done
pioneer work.

What of our own Church? Here is an item from the Laymen's Newsletter of February 1958, issued by the secretary of the Presiding Bishop's Committee on Laymen's Work: 'During the last week of October, under the joint sponsorship of the Presiding Bishop's Committee on Laymen's Work and the Woman's Auxiliary to the National Council, 34 people met for three days to consider the Ministry of the Laity in our time.' News? Indeed. This was the first time representatives of these two groups had ever met together to consider how men and women might co-operate in the essential work of the Church. Why should they? Women have their place and it is within women's groups and women's organizations; this is where they are expected to make their contribution. A woman doing her work within the sanctuary before or after service, as a member of the altar guild, is doing what a woman should do. A woman serving the priest at the altar is entirely out of place. We know that the server is a representative of the congregation, not an assistant to the priest; but if a woman should perform that representative function, it would be regarded as a threat to the apostolic order of the Church—this is much too near the function of the ministerial priesthood.

Many Church people assume, consciously or not, that man the male is intended by God to lead and govern; woman is to follow and be governed. This is thought to be the right pattern not only for the family but for the Church and society. One classic reference is Ephesians 5:22–24, part of the Gospel for the Eucharist at a marriage:

Wives be subject to your husbands, as to the Lord. For the husband is the head of the wife as Christ is the head of the Church, his body, and is himself its Saviour. As the Church is subject to Christ, so let wives also be subject in everything to their husbands.

But does this mean that all women are to be subject to all men? Can this text support a doctrine of subordination even within the marriage relationship?

There is another word of St. Paul's which must be heard: 'The wife does not rule over her own body, but the husband does; likewise the husband does not rule over his own body, but the wife does' (1 Cor. 7:4). This, without doubt, is spoken of the marriage relationship and seems to describe not subordination but mutual submission. At any rate, whatever our own interpretation of the Pauline teaching about the marriage relationship or the position of women in the Church, we have been reluctant to ask what is woman's place in the total ministry of the Church. We have not accepted women fully as persons who could make their own unique contribution as women, not denying their sex, but still as persons working as partners with men.

The whole point of what I am trying to say will be misunderstood if it is thought that the answer is the ordination of women, or even the admission of women as deputies to General Convention. This is not basically a question of status. Sherwin Bailey, writing in *Theology*, said:

What is the *whole* ministry to which God calls the *whole* Man, created in his image as a unity of male and female? There is a challenge here, not only to theological thought, but also to adventurousness in practice. . . . Woman's desire is not for the priesthood or for any ministerial status *as such*, but for acceptance into partnership with man and acknowledgment as the Other, without whom he cannot accomplish the service of God in the Church.[7]

This is the point: the acceptance of the principle that the particular and special gifts of men and of women are com-

7 S. Bailey, 'Woman and the Church's Lay Ministry,' *Theology* LVII (1954), 329-30.

plementary, to be used in partnership. The nature of the relationship of men and women derives from their relationship in Christ; it is a relationship of acceptance and appreciation, each for the other.

As I said above, the place of women in the Church is not a simple ecclesiastical matter but is part of the vast and complicated problem of the relationship between men and women in our society. But it does furnish an illustration from within our own household of the necessity of judging our corporate life in the light of the gospel.

The liturgical revival can do much not only to make us aware of the social implications of the gospel but to make them live issues for us. Just how this will show itself in the life of the Church I do not profess to know. I doubt if we shall have again in our time social action groups such as CAIL or CLID.[8] All efforts, in other Churches as well as our own, to revive such groups fail. But the felt tension must in time show itself in witness and action. We can recover the liturgy in its purest form, we can gather the people each Sunday in church for the parish Communion and lead them into the parish house for coffee and rolls. We can read the Epistle from the lectern and the Gospel from the chancel steps. We can restore the Offertory procession. We can teach the people to pray with the Church and actively to do the Eucharist. We can do all this and still fail to bring forth fruit. Robert Nelson wrote in *Parish and People* (Summer 1957):

Our attention to details of ordering services, yes, and to study of the Bible tends to make us talk and act as if these two activities are God's chief interest. That is a perilous line of development,

[8] The Church Association for the Advancement of the Interests of Labor (founded 1887); The Church League for Industrial Democracy (founded 1919).

and inevitably leads to an idolatry which one day might inspire a prophet to put into God's mouth words like these: 'I hate, I despise your parish communions and I will take no delight in your public baptisms. Yea, though ye offer me bread and wine I will not accept them: neither will I regard the corporate recitation of the Prayer of Humble Access.'

And, I think, this contemporary prophet would surely go on to repeat once more the familiar if unheeded words of Amos: 'But let justice roll down like waters and righteousness like an everflowing stream.'

I have read in Roman Catholic sources that before World War II the Nazis were not troubled about the growth of the Liturgical Movement in Germany, but rather secretly encouraged it. And we know that some of the leaders of the movement in the Roman Church, not only in Germany but in other countries of Europe, did ignore political and social problems, and even supported political programs which for every reason they should have opposed.

I cite this not as a criticism of the liturgical revival, but as an illustration of the fact that the liturgy cannot be a substitute for political wisdom or social action. When we are unaware of the social implications of the liturgy, or ignore those implications, we fail to that extent to offer ourselves to God as 'a reasonable, holy, and living sacrifice.' For each time we receive the Body and Blood of our Lord, we are by that act sent to be witnesses to Him before the world. This does not mean that we are to lead pious lives but that we are to be in the thick of the struggle for justice and freedom and peace. In the strength of Christ's victory over sin and death, we labor for the transformation of the world, knowing quite well we can never accomplish it. But we make our decisions— that is, live our faith—in the conviction that this world into which God has entered with His redeeming power will in His own time be transformed. Therefore, our labor is not in vain in the Lord. This is the hope that is our present possession in every Eucharist. This is the hope which is laid up for us in heaven.

V

THE PASTORAL IMPLICATIONS OF THE LITURGICAL RENEWAL

The Reverend John Oliver Patterson, D.D.

Rector and Headmaster of Kent School

THE PASTORAL IMPLICATIONS OF THE
LITURGICAL RENEWAL

In my instruction to speak on the pastoral implications of the liturgical renewal, I have been asked to suggest ways in which the theology and basic principles of this great stirring and ferment, this reformation of our day, may be implemented and manifested in the day by day life and work and worship of the parishes of our Church.

My assignment is on a totally different plane than that of the four men who preceded me. Their task was, in a sense, to trace the development of a satellite, to tell of its firing, and to describe its orbit. My task is perhaps to bring that satellite out of orbit, back to earth in such a way that it will not disintegrate and disappear when it comes up against the friction and hard reality of this world's atmosphere—nor land on a church and blow up the very people it is intended to inform and assist.

A return to earth somehow lacks much of the drama of the take-off. We deal less with history and research and intellectual speculation, and more with the rather drab realities of the situation at hand. 'Mystery theology' must somehow be related to an 8:00 A.M. service; the doctrine of man must somehow be applied to Mr. John Jones's specific situation; liturgical art must be thought of in terms of an existing building; and the holy fellowship, the mystical Body of Christ, in terms of St. John's or St. Paul's or Grace Church parish, its vestry, auxiliary, and men and women in the pews or absent from the pews.

I am as conscious as the next man of the dangers involved in such proceedings. I know how easy it is to become so involved with means as to forget ends. The history of the Church offers us constant warnings of the dangers of tangential excursions. That same history shows us how Christianity has suffered from the autocracy of mere priestcraft, as it has suffered from the anarchy of mere congregationalism—both well-intentioned in their beginnings. We have seen the Christian's sense of justice and corporate responsibility become perverted into 'do-goodism' or a so-called 'social gospel,' as we have at times seen the Christian sense of intellectual responsibility end in arrogance and pride.

Just so, we must never forget that the work of the liturgical renewal could become a barrier between man and God, and a cheap and facile substitute for the faith. I believe therefore that there are three great affirmations of the liturgical renewal that must always be in the forefront of our minds, and that every parochial activity must in some way and to some degree reflect these basic convictions:

First: Jesus Christ is Lord. He is the King of Glory and loyalty to Him must transcend all other loyalties of Christians.

Second: The holy Church is the earnest of His Kingdom. In the holy Church, through the gift of the Holy Spirit, Christians are to realize on earth what they will manifestly be when Christ appears in glory.

Third: The Eucharist is the great action of the Church. It is both the pleading of and the showing forth here and now of the accomplished act of redemption.

Our basic problem, then, is to find ways and means with which the parish can fulfill its vocation, as the area in which these truths are to be taught, practiced, and shown forth to the world. Our goal is that, between the present reality of our parishes and the divine ideal for our parishes, we may find techniques and policies and methods which will be effective means of joining spirit with routine activity.

The first step is to plan a type of parochial organization in which each parishioner may develop and realize a sense of being a part of the Church, a part of the holy fellowship. He has been told over and over again that by virtue of his Baptism-Confirmation he has pledged his loyalty to Christ and been incorporated into Christ's Body, with all the privileges and responsibilities that pertain thereto. And yet the average parish, as we look at the present reality offers very little opportunity for the exercise of these rights and responsibilities, little stimulus for the corporate activity of large numbers, and little if any challenge for talents. What can be done, starting from the present reality, to organize our parishes in such a way that every member in them can readily find an area in which to work—a work that needs his talent, whatever that talent may be?

One technique that is working well in many places today is the *parish council* idea. It can be dull and stupid, mere busy-work if it ever becomes an end in itself. It can be an exciting, effective technique for drawing out and expressing the loyalty and talent of every cell of the body, if it is used as a means toward the great end.

The parish council involves a group of committees to plan and carry out work in almost every aspect of parish life. A typical council might consist of from four to twelve committees, the membership of each consistent with the nature of the committee's task and proportionate to the size of the parish. The council proper consists of the clergy, wardens, and the chairman of each committee. It should meet, at least three times a year, to plan the general parish program. Particular committees should meet at least monthly. There will, of course, be variations in the number of committees in various parishes; but I suggest that as a start there should be at least committees on worship, education, evangelism, and stewardship. As the idea takes hold and the technique is understood, such committees as social relations, property, parish zoning, diocesan relations, etc. may well be added.

The council, with its committees, can say in effect to the parish: 'Here is *our* work! Here is a job for all of us. Clergy and laity alike share in a royal priesthood, a priesthood differing not in importance but in function. Our task is to make manifest our loyalty to our Lord in the divine fellowship of the parish, and, as we work, to relate all that we do to the worship of the Holy Trinity, carrying into every phase of life the grace of God given to us as we gather before His altar.'

The parish council can both induce and express the essential nature of the Church in the parish. It can bring into service large proportions of our parishioners, all sorts and kinds of talents. The details of committee-work will vary in each parish, but let me suggest a few.

Take, for example, the religious education committee. This should not be a mere amalgam of Rector and Church school superintendent, nor a mere collection of Church school teachers. It should have representation from all areas within the parish and be a planning board for *all* religious education. It could plan and sponsor the children's Church school, Confirmation classes, a school of religion for adults, educational programs for guilds, parish libraries, special interest youth groups, and educational programs for many other needs.

The committee on evangelism would have broad responsibilities: bringing to the parish the unchurched or those without specific parochial connections; seeking candidates for Baptism and Confirmation; developing ways and means of making the Church and its teaching known in the community.

One committee on stewardship of which I know shows the potential of such a group. They began by doing the usual things to assist the vestry with the Every Member Canvass. They soon shared the gloom that so often covers a vestry at that time of the year. Their unhappiness came not only from the large number of parishioners who were unwilling to make a decent pledge, or were evasive about it, but their concern stemmed from the basic attitude of so many toward money. They discussed this, searching both Scripture and tradition, until they had developed what they considered to be a fair statement of the general Christian principle of the use of money and property. They then went to the publicity committee and had them print in the parish news-sheet some summaries of their experiences and their meetings—emphasizing the Christian doctrine that money and property are not owned but are held in trust, under stewardship for which we are accountable to God and to the commonweal. This was eventually published as a booklet, with wide circulation throughout the Church. All this developed out of a committee that first thought of its work as limited to raising money for salaries and coal bill.

Particularly helpful in certain types of parishes is a council committee sometimes called the zoning committee. The name derives from the fact that many large churches have found it helpful to divide the parish into a number of geographic zones. Each zone has a group responsible for maintaining contact with the people and homes in their area. They report on illness, call to promote the general work of the parish, show the parish's interest and concern in each family. If a new family moves into the neighborhood, the clergyman can pass on information about them to the zone workers, who will call and help them get the children registered in Church school and invite them to accompany the worker to the various parochial functions. Few things can help more in sponsoring the family nature of the Church than this work, which carries it right into the homes of the people.

A committee of the council responsible for promoting good and effective relations with the Diocese can help to overcome the parochialism that marks so many places today. In one parish, where such a committee after discussion with vestry and bishop went outside what had been thought of as limits of parochial responsibility, a thorough survey was made of several areas. The committee picked out a rapidly growing suburb, and then went from door to door until they had found a large group of unchurched people. They then went to the parish council and said, 'Here are several families, unchurched, in a growing community. What shall we do?' The Christian Education Committee immediately went to work, obtained permission from the town school board to use the basement room in the community school each Sunday. They organized a Church school for children each Sunday morning and a school of religion for adults each Sunday evening.

It was a community with very little to offer by way of recreation, and so the social relations committee began to do something about this—starting with simple refreshments after the school of religion, and then providing children's parties and suppers for the whole group of these families. The committee on publicity saw to it that some of these efforts were noted in the local newspapers, with a general invitation to the community to attend the two schools. The committee on worship became concerned because nothing had been done about worship for this growing group, and so on a very simple basis services were started in the schoolhouse basement. The property committee built a small portable altar, furnished a piano, hymnals, and prayer books.

Within two years' time, a mission was organized; a church

building, seating 250, a two-story guild hall, had been built and paid for; and at the first service, the service of consecration, twelve were baptized and sixteen confirmed. It is interesting to note that the mission insisted upon the immediate necessity of a parish council for themselves. The main reason why all of this is worth telling is that 90 per cent of the work which produced this result was done by the laity of the council, not by the clergy.

In the set-up of the council proper, the wardens operate as liaison officers between council and vestry, so that any plans involving parish budget money or in any other way affecting the vestry's jurisdiction may be presented to the vestry at their regular meeting for their consideration.

Much more important than what the council and committees do is the fact that any task they do must be related to the altar and to the great action in which the parish regularly engages at that altar. In the parish, the worship of Almighty God must be primary, both in the mind of the priest and in the minds of the laity. Every project of the council, whether it be financial, social, educational, or any other, must face these questions: Is it in accord with the Church's function and goal? Is it assisting the Church to be the Church? Can it be intelligently and properly offered at the altar? All efforts of duplication or competition with civic and community organizations and efforts should be rejected. The council idea holds that the function of the Church is religious and all its activities must meet this test. We are here basically to affirm that Christ is Lord, the Church is His Body, the temple of the Holy Spirit, and its great corporate activity is the offering at which all of its life is presented at the altar in union with the eternal sacrifice of the incarnate Son.

The Church's first frontier is people. Its greatest problem today is unemployment of these people; all too few have been called to engage in the work of the Kingdom. Of course, the corporate ventures of the parish represent but one field in which such work for the Kingdom is required. But it is highly probable that if such work does not start there, it will not be found starting in the office, home, factory, or farm.

Does this sound like busy work, a program of activism? The facts contend otherwise. Until we have set up the kind of parish in which each member has a chance really to be a parishioner, we are not going to get very far. The Church is a family; a family is a corporate venture with place for, work for, love for, each. Until we have faced fairly and squarely the nature and function of the parish, we cannot successfully move forward in our work. Of course, it is in worship that the parish finds its real reason for existence and expresses most fully its true nature. It is in worship that the individual is brought to the source of all grace. Worship is the mainspring of all Christian living, for only in worship do we find the center of life outside ourselves.

In many cases this tremendous responsibility upon our parishes calls for an examination and re-evaluation of many traditions long accepted as normal. Just as we must rethink our techniques of organization and administration, so that our parishes will show a sound doctrine of the Church, so we must rethink the whole matter of 'common prayer' so that our services will reflect what both Scripture and tradition agree to be the Christian liturgy.

The most obvious place to begin such an evaluation is with the very building where worship takes place. Church buildings should be outward and visible signs of our inward spirit and tradition. First of all, we must remember that the beauty of a house of God will not be determined on superficial aesthetic grounds only. Christian beauty must always reflect Christian use. Our church buildings should clearly show forth that they are above all else a place of sacrifice where a congregation can gather at the altar of God.

If we look to the history of the architectural setting of Anglicanism, we will find that our classic principle of ecclesiology is that both for the sacraments and for other offices the altar and the officiant must be placed in close relationship to the people. In a building that attempts to be true to the best in the Anglican tradition, everything should be subordinated to this principle, for on its successful realization depends that congregational liturgical worship which is the aim, and the glory, of the Book of Common Prayer.

Over the centuries, three different types of altars have been developed in Christianity: the mysterious, the dramatic, and the ministerial. There is the altar of Eastern Christianity, the mysterious altar; there is the dramatic altar of the baroque architects and of the Victorian ritualists; and there is the ministerial altar, the holy Table of the apostolic Church.[1] It is this last, the altar of ministering, where our Lord perpetuates His ministry here on earth, which best represents the ethos and ideal of the religion of the Prayer Book. It is to the loss and detriment of our Church that we have so largely discarded this type of altar and the building appropriate to it.

This is not to blind us to certain values in the two other types, the mysterious and the dramatic. There is value in the use of drama and of the building that expresses the mystery and splendor of Christian worship. But to give priority to the ministerial principle, both in altars and buildings, need never be done at the cost of drama and mystery. On the other hand, when in history priority has been given to the dramatic and

---

[1] For this distinction, I am indebted to G. W. O. Addleshaw and F. Etchells, *The Architectural Setting of Anglican Worship* (Faber and Faber, 1948), p. 200.

mysterious, it would seem that the ministerial principle has been lost.

I realize that there are people who express the fear that if the altar stands near the congregation, the congregation may lose a sense of awe and reverence which can be produced by the more dramatic altar located at the end of a dark, mysterious church. This could be; but I deny emphatically that it need be. If the ministerial type of altar, preferably free standing and so situated that the congregation can clearly see and join in the liturgy, is dignified in itself and in its few and simple ornaments, then any danger can be completely avoided, without sacrificing the very important ministerial factor. Needless to say, such a statement assumes the same kind of dignity and planning in the matter of ceremonial. And I do insist that this matter of architecture is of far more than superficial importance. I emphasize our obligation to build new churches and to remodel our existing churches in such a way as to recapture the basic tradition not only of our own Anglican communion but of apostolic Christianity—a tradition concerned with the very nature of the Church and its liturgy.

The same responsibility rests upon us in lesser areas of liturgical art. It may be that only a few of us will have a chance to build a new church, but many of us will have chances to remodel, and all of us have the opportunity at least to cleanse the present temple. Using your parish council property committee (if they represent converted people, as they should), go into the church and clear out everything you can that does not contribute to clarity, simplicity, and joyfulness in the structure. Whenever you find it possible to sneak a 'gadget' off the altar, do so. The one real ornament of the altar is the Eucharist. We might use the same policy with some of the pictures so often found hanging in parish houses and Church school rooms. Tawdry art, bad ventilation, poor illumination, and pale-hued representations of hyper-thyroid angels, are not compatible with the religion of Christ who is Light of Light!

When we look to the Sunday worship in the majority of parishes in the Church, we find that the only common denominator seems to be the early (7:30 or 8:00 A.M.) celebration of the Eucharist, found in most places where there is a resident priest. It is the Lord's own service on the Lord's own day—but it would be difficult and scarcely true to say that the congregation represents the Lord's own people in the parish at common prayer. In the majority of cases, it represents a very small proportion of the congregation—at best the saints of the parish, at worst a self-conscious, divisive group.

If the principal service at 11:A.M. is a celebration of the Holy Eucharist, as it is in an increasing number of parishes, one of two problems immediately arises. If it is a non-communicating celebration, then it violates the historic tradition of the Church, concealing as it does the wholeness of the Eucharistic action with its great climax in the actual reception of the Holy Communion. The non-communicating celebration is a partial truth, and partial truths are always dangerous. If it is a celebration of the Eucharist with communions, it provokes a rather difficult problem for many whose devotional and disciplinary life calls upon them to fast before communion, a practice with the staunch support of the Church's tradition. Such fasting is more than a petty problem of fancy piety. It is a practice embodying a principle enjoined upon Christians to save them from falling into slothfulness, irreverence, and unthinking, casual reception of the Holy Communion. While the technique and details of such fasting are of relatively small importance, the principle involved is not.

In many parishes, the 'principal' service is Morning Prayer.

There are a great many good things to be said about Morning Prayer. I, for one, believe it should be offered as a public service every day in every parish as the Prayer Book suggests. Yet we are all aware of the fact that today fewer and fewer people of any school of thought or churchmanship look upon Morning Prayer as the full, normal expression of the Church's life and worship. Most are agreed that it is not the desired norm for Sunday.

Over against this picture of the general Sunday practice of our Church today, we must again set the ideal: the norm of worship is the Lord's own service for the Lord's own people on the Lord's own day. The Lord's Supper is of divine institution. In the holy gospel Christ did 'command us to continue a perpetual memory of that His precious death and sacrifice until His coming again.' The Eucharist is an expression in words and action of the gospel of the Lord. If the worship in our parishes fails to show this unmistakably, then we are not meeting our great responsibility. Our third affirmation is that the Eucharist is both the pleading of and the showing forth here and now of the accomplished act of redemption. The Eucharist is the great Sunday act of worship for the Church.

We must be certain that to the best of our ability the Eucharist is presented in such a way that it is clearly seen for what it is and has been. No teaching or presentation of its action which would reduce it to a service of fellowship, or a mere 'memorial of the Passion,' or no more than a 'means of communion,' will be anything other than a partial truth. The Eucharist must not be *used*. We must think very carefully before we celebrate it as the 'opening exercise' for group meetings, or subscribe to the idea of a 'children's Eucharist,' or support a 'daily mass' merely for the sake of having a daily mass. Equally, of course, we must be very careful of the kind of rationalization which attempts to excuse a scarcity of cele-brations by talking about something 'too sacred to be used with frequency.'

The doctrine is that the Eucharist is the Catholic (i.e. the universal), durable, and common act of the Body of Christ. The elements of bread and wine are to be presented; the invocation of God does obey His command and corresponds to His will; the elements do undergo His preoccupation; and the original actuality of the death of the Saviour in some way exists among the faithful. By virtue of that death, we com-municate upon Him living.

It is important also to remember what has been called the true 'domestic character' of the Eucharistic worship. The Church is the household of faith, the family of God. The fam-ily of the Blood of Christ has, as has every family, one par-ticular time and place and act by which its integrity is most fully realized, its standards revealed, its purpose expressed, and its strength restored. That is in the family meal, the covenant feast. In that meal, the family shows forth its origin and destination, its purpose and the source of its power. It is with the Church, even as with our own particular human families—father, mother, children, all have the privilege and responsibility of the family meal; and all recognize, con-sciously or unconsciously, that here is the family in its purest function, feeding body, mind, and spirit. Thus the full expres-sion of the Eucharist is possible only when priest and laymen alike take full part and give full offering and response.

I do not need to say that this is not always the case. We know how easy it is for a congregation to degenerate into a kind of appendix, letting the choir and clergy carry on the worship. We all know parishes where the congregation some-times comes to church as though daring the preacher to move them with a sermon and the choir to entertain them. We know parishes where congregational participation in public worship seems to be looked upon as a happily decreasing phenomenon. What we must strive for is that the parish restore to its fullness that which we see now only in part—true common prayer, real liturgical worship, a truly corporate response on the part of the Church in the parish to God's gracious revelation of Himself. Of course, this requires a great deal of sound teaching. Any successful corporate activity needs some measure of corporate understanding. Our parishes, our people, need to be brought to a realization of what the Eucharist means; they will most effectively grasp this when they have some understanding of what the Eucharist is!

This can be glibly said—but it touches upon what might be called a heresy in our day. For a number of people of all schools of churchmanship, the Eucharist is a service that is said in church by a priest. One notes in common language that the Catholic-minded clergyman says, 'I am going to say Mass'; the Evangelically minded clergyman says, 'I am going to take the early service.' More is involved than a mere bickering over terms. It is part of a large body of evidence pointing to a rather common misconception of sacramental theology in our day—a misconception that explains why so many people think of worship not in corporate terms, not even in terms of personal religion, but rather as private religion. This is the very antithesis of true worship. One of the great tasks before us today is to restore to our people an understanding of the Eucharist as something given and done rather than as something heard and felt. The early Christian did not say, 'I am going to church'; he said, 'I am going to offer, going to sacrifice.' For him the first great thought about this Eucharist was his self-offering, to give himself over into God's possession.

The Eucharist is not something a priest says; the Eucharist is something the Church does. The part played by the laity in a celebration is just as significant as that played by the clergy, however it may differ. Clement of Rome in the first century reminded Christians that each is to 'make Eucharist according to his own order.'[2] All orders, whether of layman, priest, or bishop, have their particular ministry without which the worship of the Church is incomplete.

If the Eucharist is to become the regular, normative, corporate act of Sunday worship for the parish, then we must be thoroughly realistic in selecting an hour for that service. Many parishes all over the country are finding that 9:00 or 9:30 A.M. offers many advantages. Where a parish presently has the 11:00 A.M. Morning Prayer tradition, many find that it is advantageous to introduce a parish Eucharist at an earlier hour as a supplement to, rather than a substitute for, the 11:00 A.M. service. In some situations, this would be the effective way to work, not cutting out the established Morning Prayer at the later hour, nor penalizing people by the rigors of the early 7:30 or 8:00 A.M. hour.

But before we discuss further considerations of the hour, let us deal a little with this question of Morning Prayer versus the Eucharist as the service of the day; for many people are disturbed at the thought of a change from Morning Prayer to Holy Communion. This does not mean that all of them are protesting the Eucharist; many of them are truly and sincerely attached to Morning Prayer and find real value in it. In this they show good judgment. The Psalms, Old Testament lessons, and canticles, are precious parts of the Christian heritage. The priest or parish that washes them out of the picture is making a serious mistake. Yet we recognize the priority of the Eucharist. What can be done?

First of all, there is a partial solution to be found in the use of the Offices daily. Certainly that is the standard set by the

[2] I Clement 41:1.

Prayer Book. But the Prayer Book goes further and proposes in its rubrics that there is a combination of Morning Prayer and the Lord's Supper that brings to the sacrament the most important elements of the Office. Moreover it is a service which can show forth the ministry of the laity, for the Morning Prayer sections can be conducted entirely by lay readers and choir. The service begins with the Sentences, passes to the Versicles and *Venite*, uses the Psalms and an Old Testament lesson. Following the lesson, one of the canticles serves as an Introit for the procession of the celebrant and his assistants who approach the altar to begin the Eucharist. Such a service requires but little more time and recaptures for the great Sunday service the Psalms and Old Testament lections.

To return to the question of an earlier hour for the principal service—Sunday is as a rule the only day for family fellowship and recreation. The 9:00 or 9:30 hour for church gives families a longer day together than when church lasts till noon or later. Except in very affluent parishes, the earlier hour means that Sunday noon meal is no longer an excuse for the absence of the hard-working housewife. It means that without undue hardship the congregation can receive the Holy Communion fasting, and that they have come to church fairly soon after arising, rather than after breakfast, dishwashing, the Sunday paper, and a TV show. This is a decided help, if we are to be realistic about men's attitudes and the place they play in worship.

Moreover it means that children can once again be treated as churchmen and not as strange little beings for whom a new religion is invented. For a parish communion is not a true parish communion unless the youth of the parish be included —at least those old enough to last through an hour long service, the younger ones being dismissed perhaps after the Creed to go to class for instruction. At any rate, the earlier service offers opportunity for all to come to the church together. Perhaps, in parishes where it can be done, a better plan is for the Church school to meet on Saturday. More and more parishes are discovering that Episcopalians, even as Lutherans and others, can be reached on Saturday for a full hour of teaching. In this way, the 9:00 or 9:30 hour for the principal parish worship on Sunday could mean that children of fourth-grade age and older would attend church with their parents, becoming familiar with the Eucharist, and restoring the family pew idea. Since the whole family would come to church together, the younger kindergarten and primary age would have classes in the parish house. All children fourth grade and older would receive their instruction either on Saturdays, or, in those places where it is possible, through the school 'released time' plan.

A further advantage of the earlier hour is that it gives opportunity for a parish breakfast after the service. The parish family-unity achieved and expressed in the service is not to be neglected as soon as the service is over. A simple breakfast in the guild hall or parish house, reminiscent of the Agape of the early Church, can be a real continuation of the fellowship of the altar; and many will testify that it far outweighs guild meetings, tea parties, and other programs as a realistic means of strengthening and expressing friendship and corporate life within the parish.

The same kind of appraisal should be made of the hour of other services of the parish. It is difficult, for example, to teach Baptism as the initiatory rite into the fellowship and body of the Church, if that holy sacrament is administered at 3:00 P.M. in a dark corner of an empty church. It seems rather tragic to preach and teach a sacramental religion, and then not offer our people a real and regular chance to practice it. It is wrong to pledge allegiance to our Lord Christ and then not obey His command: 'Do this.' It is futile for us to speak of the Eucharist as the corporate action of the whole Christian body and then not present that action in such a way that all can take full part. We must bring our parishes back to a realization that the church building is by definition 'a roof over an altar' and that the liturgy of that altar is the essential work of the holy Church of God who is sovereign of all creation.

The starting point for the theology of the parish is the realization that a parish is not composed of buildings, endowments, mortgages, or traditions. A parish is composed of people, people who through Baptism-Confirmation have undertaken a new relationship with God. This new relationship, this new covenant, means, in the words of St. Peter, that these people are to be 'an holy priesthood, to offer up spiritual sacrifices, acceptable to God by Jesus Christ' (I Pet. 2:5). This teaching has been fundamental in Christianity, and for 1900 years the Church has insisted upon the essential oneness of Christian living and Christian worship. Our parishes are here to present to all the two great foundations, the Bible and the Eucharist, the uttered word and the living presence, the holy doctrine and the holy food. The goal toward which we strive is that week by week the men and women of the Church join in offering their 'bounden duty and service,' the offering of praise and thanksgiving. Equally, all else that goes on in the parish must be measured by the extent to which it is related to the altar and expresses the Christian teaching that all of life is to be offered to God for its redemption. Yet this can end up as nothing more than vague idealism if it is not made clear and real at the time and place and action of the sacrifice. The very nature of a sacrament demands from us tremendous concern and reverence for the outward and visible aspects of that sacrament, for the when, where, who, and how, as they might be called.

To continue our thinking about a few of the things that can be done and taught to bring before our people an understanding of the action, we suggest some matters that can be done and taught in any kind of parish, whether one accustomed to a Solemn High Mass or one where celebrant wears a Geneva gown. We are concerned here with fundamentals that cut across all party lines and all partisan thinking in the field of ceremonial. Let me suggest a few, starting with the lesser, moving on to the more important:

1. Constantly present the actual structure of the Eucharist —the skeleton or shape of the liturgy—to the people in such a way that they can grasp it. Many parishes use a printed or mimeographed Sunday announcement sheet with hymn numbers and so forth. You can outline the service for them clearly on these, perhaps listing the action under five heads including a prologue and epilogue:

The Preparation (through the sermon)
The Offertory (through the Confession)
The Consecration (through Lord's Prayer)
The Communion
The Thanksgiving [3]

2. Give careful consideration to the actors in the drama, for such it is in the most reverent sense. Little boys as servers may touch the hearts of mothers, but I doubt if they are the best representatives at the altar of the ministry of laymen. Use men as servers, keeping boys for other acolyte tasks, and by men I mean adults who are truly representative of the Church in the parish.

[3] Suggestive ideas following this outline will be found in the brochure of the Associated Parishes, *The Parish Eucharist*.

3. Let the servers, by their posture during the service, clearly portray the nature of their ministry. They are not simply extra hands for the celebrant; they have a real function in the sacrifice, they are the *circumstantes*.[4] Therefore, they should stand along with the celebrant throughout most of the service, kneeling only for the Confession and Absolution, the Prayer of Humble Access and the reception of Communion, and the final Blessing. This can vividly teach the corporate nature of the rite and keep the celebrant from dominating the scene.

4. The hymns used should be of the objective type, centered in God and in the Church's faith and work. Subjective, individualistic hymns are unworthy of the Eucharist. Hymns and anthems should, of course, be related to the propers of the day and season, and the general music of the service should be such as the congregation can learn and sing.

5. The sermon should be liturgical, that is, related to the propers of the day. The preacher's task is to proclaim the gospel, and the Church has given us a balanced presentation of that gospel in the assigned propers of the Prayer Book. Moreover, a parish Eucharist should not be thought of as an occasion for cutting down on the sermon and substituting a 'prone' or a simple little instruction. This is to be the major worship activity of the parish and should be treated as such. The Church stands on the double foundation, the Bible and the Eucharist, the holy doctrine and the holy food, the uttered word and the living presence.

6. There is real advantage in a Gospel procession. It can be as simple or as elaborate as is desired, but there is great teaching value in having the Book brought down from the

---

[4] 'Those standing around'—a term from the Roman Canon of the Mass.

altar to the people and the Gospel lesson proclaimed to the Church. The world—indeed often the Church—does not know that Gospel, and we greatly need to emphasize and dignify its presentation. Widespread evidence testifies that the procession is an effective technique toward this end.

7. A most valuable means of teaching one important meaning of the Eucharist is the Offertory procession, a restoration of a usage of the Church for many centuries. Here again is something that can be done with simplicity or with great ceremonial, depending upon the parish setting. It makes little difference as to the amount of ceremonial used; it is the fundamental action that counts. We give a brief description of this action as it is done in many parishes:

Before service, the altar guild places the bread box and cruets on a table or shelf at the back of the church, preferably at the end of the center aisle where the communicants can see them as they enter the church. Often they can effectively be placed near the font and thus make one more reminder to the people that everything that we are and desire (for such is represented by the elements) is to be baptized into Christ and united to His self-offering. Immediately after the Offertory Sentence, and when the hymn or anthem begins and the ushers start receiving the alms, the crucifer goes quietly down a side aisle to the back of the church. There the procession is formed, after alms are received—crucifer and torchbearers (if they are a part of the parish ceremonial tradition), two ushers with the alms, and two with the elements. The procession goes up the aisle to the sanctuary gate. The priest and servers, or deacon if desired, meet them, receive the alms, prepare the paten, and go to the altar to offer it. The same is done with the chalice.

God's revelation has brought man's response. 'What reward shall I give unto the Lord for all the benefits that He has done unto me?' (Psalm 116:11). Nothing less than the whole of life is worthy of offering to Him who has revealed Himself so fully in answer to man's need. Thus it is that the congregation bring forward first their alms, tokens of their labor, and then bread and wine, food and drink, the essentials of life, as their offering in response. These elements are symbols of the whole of man—ourselves, our souls and bodies, freely and willingly and morally offered to God. They represent our joys, our sorrows, our sins and virtues, our hopes, our failures, our sickness and health—the whole of each communicant offered at the altar. They are wheat and grapes, and as such they represent also the whole creation. But note that it is creation with man's work added to it, and so they represent God's world and what man has done to it and with it. All that goes to make up life, the life of the individual worshipper, the life of the worshipping community, and the life of the world today, is involved in this offering as it is lifted before God's altar, offered for redemption even as it is offered in recognition that God is the creator, owner, and giver of all. The Church stands reverently and silently as the oblation is presented.

These few suggestions for a more effective presentation of the Eucharist, techniques supported by centuries of Christian usage and increasingly used in our Church today, can make in their proper, intelligent use all the difference between sterility and virility in our parish worship.

The great act of offering, consecration, and communion is the true expression of what the Church is and is to be. The Eucharist is in a sense both the beginning and the ending of Christian living, a circle encompassing the whole of life. We might draw such a circle representing the life of the parish and thus of every parishioner for a week. A tiny arc on the circumference of that circle would represent the parish

Eucharist—one extreme labeled 9:00 A.M. Sunday, the other 10:00 A.M. or whatever figure indicates the actual service. The tag over the whole arc is 'Our Parish Eucharist.'

But is this quite true? Does the Eucharist begin with the processional hymn or the Collect for Purity? Does it not begin with the work of the altar guild preparing the sanctuary and the vessels? Or, on Saturday, with the sexton's work in cleaning the church, or the rector's work in preparing himself for the celebration? Perhaps we should extend the length of the arc on the circle so that it reads 9:00 A.M. Saturday to 10:00 A.M. Sunday. But just as the altar guild is truly participating in the sacrifice of the altar by preparing the elements, so those who grew the wheat and those who made the bread, those who pressed the grapes and those who transported the wine, participate in the sacrifice also and are offered at the altar.

So also each parishioner is participating in the Eucharistic action, which is to include the offering of himself, his soul and body, on Friday at his work, on Thursday in his play, on Wednesday in his home, on Tuesday in his solitude, on Monday in his sickness. For the offering is to be a complete offering, a whole offering; and the bread and wine we present are true symbols of that whole offering. We offer the wages that we pay employees, the codes by which we compete in business, the things we do behind locked doors. We offer Him the world's statesmanship, and the world's carnage, the young man's visions and the old man's dreams. And so with each phase of our existence, the time tag on the arc labeled Eucharist is pushed further and further back, until it has completed the whole circumference of the circle, and all of life is seen to be Eucharistic. For such it is. Every thought and word and deed is to be brought to the altar, united to Christ's eternal offering, and presented to our heavenly Father. All of life for the Christian must be liturgy.

When we have regained an understanding of the liturgy and of its implications, we will have unleashed the most potent, effective, and God-given weapon we have for the conversion of the world. When we have done so, we will be obedient to our commission in the world. When we have done so, we can then put aside all our failing techniques, our frantic appeals, for it is basically in the Eucharist that we shall find motive and power for Christian living. For the Eucharist is the Lord's gift of Himself, that His people may be so fully united to Him that it is not only they alone that live, but He lives in them—that they 'might bear about in the body the dying of the Lord Jesus, that the life also of Jesus might be manifest in that body' (2 Cor. 4:10).

VI

THE WORD FOR ASCENSIONTIDE

A SERMON

The Reverend William Hamilton Nes,
D.D., D.C.L., LL.D.

*Professor of Homiletics,
Seabury-Western Theological Seminary*

THE WORD FOR ASCENSIONTIDE

In the Name of the Father, and of the Son,
and of the Holy Ghost. Amen.

The things which are to be spoken now are not easily ar-
ranged. They are for me profoundly urgent to be said. Therefore I must at the beginning ask your forgiveness if they do
not have that artfulness of transition and of form which perhaps a sermon ought always to have. If I may use Father
Patterson's space travel analogy, I must tell you that I expect
that you will have some bumpiness when the several stages
of my rocket disengage. Nevertheless, I shall do the best I can
to make you as comfortable as possible.

The first of the things I wish to speak about concerns this
day in Ascensiontide. We may ask: What is the word for
today? What is the word for this season, which is completed
tomorrow in the Octave? The word, of course, is Glory. Our
Lord was received into the Glory; and out of the Glory He
shall come. This is one of the beautiful, splendid images of
Biblical typology.

I do not know (nor does anyone else), beyond what is said
so briefly in the New Testament, what the Apostles saw.
I cannot believe that they are inventing mythology. At the
same time, what they saw was naïvely said. It has come
to us through a tradition which was already formed when the
records were written. If they saw mist upon the mountain,
and when it departed He was departed, it still remains a fact

149

that our Lord has been received into the Shekinah, because in some ultimate reality He is the Shekinah, the Glory of God.

And into the cloud He went and in the cloud He will come. This is the Glory of the Lord and it is also the Glory of human destiny. The physical emergence of man in this universe from a cold hydrogen cloud, incredible numbers of years ago, a cloud spontaneously generated as they say, does not preclude the possibility that man has within him spirit, endowed by God. And it does mean that man is involved in the cosmic process of which, in terms of the process, he is a product. So the question is always before man: Who am I, where do I go? What is the creation for, and where does it go? This, in the Christian Gospel, is summed up in the word that Destiny is Glory. For the Son of Man shall present the saints of the Most High, and with them the destiny of the creation for which it was made in goodness, to Him that sitteth upon the throne, the Ancient of Days.

That this is faith received, who would deny? But I think it is necessary that we should recognize that, while we all believe it, we believe it dimly. We live in the time (and perhaps all times are like this in one way or another) in which it is possible to slide off, little by little, into the maximizing shadows of a diminished light toward a practical or even theoretical atheism. It is necessary sometimes to see a thing over against what it is not. Therefore I wish that we should recognize the infirmity of our own faith, but be encouraged and fortified by perceiving quite clearly what the alternative is.

I wish to speak now of something about which I must again try to allay your apprehension and arouse the feelings of patience which I need; for I am going to speak very briefly of the Theravada Buddhist doctrine. I am not taking you around the world on a Cook's tour of comparative religion. But we are confronted in America in this post-Christian age, if it is that, as Toynbee calls it, with a time of shadow, when we do not necessarily perceive clearly, because of all the gradations of slipping that stand in between our own faith and what the alternative is. Indeed a good deal of the disregard of God, practical and theoretical, which is about us, is a precipitated and rather jejune interpretation of the meaning of science. It is not indigenous to our culture. It pops up from time to time in a sort of protest or rebellion against dogma or the Church, or many other factors.

I want you to see the alternative in its fully thought out form. The Theravada doctrine of Buddhism, which I believe to be the authentic and primitive Buddhism, insists not only that there is no God but that there cannot be a God. To quote one of the modern interpreters of Buddhism from within Buddhism (and this is as far as I wish to go into reference): 'He that takes refuge in Buddha must not do it in the blind faith that Buddha can save him, Buddha can point the way, but he cannot walk in it for you.' This is the alternative to the words 'I am the Way, and the Truth, and the Life; abide in me, as I abide in you.'

One of the particular values, I think, of seeing the alternative is that it is fully thought out. It represents 2500 years of thinking out. It is in many ways more noble than the atheisms, practical and theoretical, which flank our own faith in our culture and in our time. It recognizes two things that are unalterable, which a good deal of modern Western atheism does not recognize: That there is the reality of the way things are, the law which has moral implications for man—the *dharma*; and that there is a force, called tamic force, of cause and effect, so that in the existential moment—which is the only reality of man's cognition—the past is always flowing into the future, and yet flowing into it by modification of one's acts and thoughts. But all this is a cyclical movement, the birth and rebirth, not of the same essence, but one candle when it is extinguished lights another.

Now here is something thoroughgoing enough, sure enough, and in its way noble enough, for us to see where the difference is. It means that there is no possibility of any help at all except such modest help as one wayfarer may give to another, if it does not too greatly disturb the detachment of his own pilgrimage. It means, however, not merely that there is nothing which can give us protection or strength or destiny, but it means also that we have no one to whom to pray. And that is the thing we must think about, lest our religion be a merely selfish, infantile search for someone to mother us or father us, however real and ultimate such a need actually is. It is necessary for us that we should admire, as well as use, even nature. And if there is no God, then all that man can admire or praise are such gods as he can find, or in a prolonged renunciation and a long good-bye, to admire nature as it is and the reality as it is. But it is always moving away from him and he from it.

While ours is a culture not at all controlled by the Theravada doctrine of Buddhism, there is in modern literature and poetry this renunciation and despair.

> I knew a lady of the west country,
>   Fair of face and form was she,
> She was the most beautiful lady
>   That ever lived in the west country.
>
> But beauty vanishes—beauty passes
>   However rare, rare it be.
> And when I crumble, who will remember
>   This lady from the west country?

Your choice, nor mine, is not to be between faith and half-faith, for you cannot play this game with half-measures. Your choice *must be* (and it *is*) a choice of faith. It is a choice of commitment; it is a choice of risking the complete investment of all you have and all you cherish. And for Christians in faith, the word for today is not an interminable cycle of one universe being born out of the debris of another and making a new debris for yet another and another, nor is it the wheel of time, nor is it the despair of the godless. The word for today is Glory—Glory into which we are permitted and called to share.

The second thing of which I wish to speak is that Ascensiontide moves to Whitsunday. This is a strange and beautiful tide. The apostles and first Christians, when the crucifixion occurred, were smitten with a shock of disillusionment and despair, and they said: 'This was He whom we *had thought* would redeem Israel.' He was gone, and when the cloud again received Him, He was gone too—but they did not withdraw into disillusionment and fear. They returned to Jerusalem, praising and glorifying God.

And then they had to wait. They did not know really what it was they were waiting for. They had experienced a rebuke of their own most wistful hope, 'Dost thou at this time restore the kingdom to Israel?' Yet in joy, in a regal exaltation that completely controlled them, they were waiting for something they did not yet comprehend, for a time which they did not know the length of. And when the Holy Spirit came, they were empowered to go into the world to proclaim that the destiny is indeed Glory, for they had seen the risen Christ—not as a ghost, not as a spirit, not as a resuscitated man, but risen from the empty tomb and 'seen of Cephas, then of the Twelve, then of five hundred brethren at once of whom the greater part remain until now, then of James, then of all the apostles, and last of all,' says Paul, 'as of one untimely born, by me.'

This was what they went out with: 'Christ died for our sins according to the Scriptures and He was buried. And He was raised the third day according to the Scriptures and He was *seen.*' Now the Holy Spirit has come into the Church, once for all. This is one of those realities, revelations. We have not to summon the Holy Spirit down from above. The Holy Spirit is in us as well as with us. Yet here is one of the many dialectical paradoxes of the faith, that while the Holy Spirit is come, the Holy Spirit comes—

> Come Holy Ghost, our souls inspire,
> And lighten with celestial fire:

The first and completely positive, unalterable coming of the Holy Ghost launched the mission of the Church into all the world: To break down every barrier that distinguishes between men except that distinction which men alone can make among themselves—the distinction of whether or not they will accept the Gospel; to break down the wall of partition between Jew and Gentile, that all the nations should become the people of God.

There is in St. Paul's epistles a phrase that I will not now attempt to exegete. I want to leave it with you as something so splendid and magnificent that you can meditate on it for a long time. He speaks of the work of the apostolate—his and that of the Church—as a *hierourgia* that the oblation of the Gentiles might be sanctified with Holy Spirit (Romans 15: 16). This, of course, leads us to the Liturgical Movement, and yet I am not going to speak of that except very briefly at the end.

However, there is something here so magnificent that I hope you will think and pray about it and meditate upon it, because notwithstanding that the Holy Spirit is here—that the Holy Spirit sanctifies the sacraments, sanctifies the Church, sanctifies you—He is come, never to be taken from us. He is come, in that striking phrase of Bishop Gore, not to compensate the absence of Christ but to accomplish His presence.

This is true. And yet we must always pray that the Holy Spirit shall come; for the Holy Spirit is always coming, though He is always here. As God has created once, yet 'my Father worketh hitherto and I work.' Christ has come; He will come. He comes at the altar; He comes into your heart; He comes to people who have never known Him. Do not fret about these dialectical differences of words. You know what the truth is: that the activity, the dynamic of the eternal reality of God's dealing with us cannot be said in a single phrase. He has created; He creates. He has redeemed; He redeems. He has sanctified; He sanctifies. He has come; He will come, and He comes.

I venture to propound to you something that is taking form in my own heart. I want to put it to you first in its threat. In its threat, let us face it. Unless the Church embarks upon a new and genuine missionary confrontation of the new global world with the gospel, Christianity will be relegated by its own adherents, so far as *they* are concerned, to being the function of an obsolete society. Today, as in the case of the apostles, it is necessary that Christianity shall not be left only to those who *were* the chosen people. We are the new Israel.

It is my belief that, while I am not a starry-eyed ecumenist, the Ecumenical Movement has not yet fully understood itself in its implications. It often seems to me, in my associations with it—which have been numerous—to have its vision warped, to be myopic, as though the only thing that could be done is somehow to resolve the denominational differences of Protestantism. With that, certainly, Anglicans cannot at all concur. But in any case, whatever its limitations, whatever its defects of consciousness, I am certain in the conviction that is growing in me that God is calling the Church, in some outpouring of God the Holy Ghost in our time, to confront new cultures, to be aware of itself *as the Church*, to move by its own spontaneous expansion into a new immersion and involvement in the new societies that are being born. And it cannot do this unless there is some measure of integration in the doing of it.

Therefore, look at the Liturgical Movement, look at the Ecumenical Movement, and then see them both as some stirring of the Spirit all-holy in the Body of Christ, which humanly looks so utterly incapable of being really the Body of Christ, for some adventure that shall mean our commitment to the Lord Jesus Christ, that His gospel is for all men, everywhere, and at all times—on no other terms, than the terms of the Church itself. There is, therefore, neither Jew nor Greek, there is neither bond nor free, male nor female, barbarian nor Scythian, but a new creature. And *this* is the word for the waiting time. For what is to be done, we, no more than the apostles in a similar time, have it in us to do, except as God with His fire and His wind takes hold of us and makes of us what He wishes us to be.

And so, in conclusion, there is certainly no more ultimate reason for the mission of the Church than that all men shall know who He is who has saved them—shall know that the destiny is Glory, and shall know what it is to find some transcendent Reality, vertically entering into life to change it and them.

There are two words so much used by the Eastern Orthodox theologians, I wish we ourselves in the West could see them and feel them more. They are the words 'transformation' and 'transfiguration.' It is only to the transformed man that the world is transfigured. And so the Liturgical Movement represents for me, among other things, this: that the end result, that the mission of the Church in this world, is to bring all men into the Eucharistic fellowship, that they may have God to praise, that they may find that He alone is worthy of the praise that rises to the lips as the sun touches the top of a mountain or the waves of the sea or the face of a loved one.

The creature is to be glorified in the glory of God, and only in God can anything find itself. And it is in the Eucharist and in the Eucharistic fellowship—the eschatological Eucharistic fellowship—that the reality of the Church is set forth and made. For there we praise; there we offer that only offering perfect in His eyes, the one true, pure, immortal sacrifice of our Lord Jesus Christ. There we receive the food of wayfarers, which is the Body and Blood of Christ. What is it but the receiving of the Body of Christ, within the Body of Christ, to become the Body of Christ. Again, this is dialectical paradox, but every soul here knows interiorly what it is: 'Ye are one Body because ye eat of one bread; and ye are one Body by the work of one Spirit.' You are all sons of one Father; you are saved by one eternal and loving Saviour who gave His life for us.

What is it to be the Body of Christ? To be the Body of Christ is to walk the dusty roads of compassion, to make no peace with oppression, to be clothed like the penitent witnesses in the Revelation, with sackcloth for our own sins, and to preach with joy that these sins are removable and have been removed by Jesus Christ for us and for all men by the one redemption which He wrought. To be the Body of Christ is to bear His Cross. And every Christian death—and death is for all of us—is a martyrdom and a dying with Christ, if we would offer it with all the rest of our life to Him. And so to be the Body of Christ is to live with Him, to die with Him, to be raised by Him through the power of Holy Spirit to the glory of God the Father. Amen.

INDEX

Absolution, 83, 91, 94, 95

Altar, 109, 131-2

Anamnesis, 5, 6, 16, 34

Anglicans, 10, 16, 17, 28, 29, 30, 41, 45-50, 59, 63-4, 65, 67, 70, 72, 73-4, 77, 90-91, 113, 114, 115-16, 139, 156

Architecture, 45-6, 65, 109, 130-31

Art, liturgical, 8-9, 35, 39, 45-6, 49, 61, 64-6, 131-3

Baptism, 6, 8, 83, 91, 93, 94, 105-6, 109, 110, 112, 125, 139

Baptists, 41, 66

Beauduin, L., 30-31

Bible translations, 38-9

Biblical theology, 8-9, 50, 114

Book of Common Prayer, 4, 47-9, 72, 73, 77, 90, 131, 134, 137-8; revisions of, 47-8

Bouyer, L., 30, 46, 101

Brilioth, Y., 10, 42, 85

Buddhism, 150-52

Calvinists, *see* Reformed Churches

Casel, O., 4-6, 11-12, 26, 32-4

Centre de Pastorale Liturgique, 39-40

Church School, 62, 126, 139

Church Year, 7-8, 37, 70, 76

Common Service Book, 43, 73, 86, 90

Congregationalists, 41, 50, 58, 67

Cullmann, O., 30, 45

Dialogue Mass, 31, 38

Dix, G., 12, 30, 33, 34, 48

Eastern Orthodox Churches, 10, 33, 52, 89, 131

Ecumenical Movement, 21, 50-51, 73, 75, 81-2, 114, 115, 155-6

Epiclesis, 8, 90, 135

Episcopalians, *see* Anglicans

Eucharist, 5-7, 8, 10-13, 14-17, 31, 33-4, 37-8, 42, 44, 46, 49, 52, 72, 74, 78, 83, 90-91, 93, 94-5, 96-7, 104, 109, 110, 112, 118-19, 120, 124, 132, 133-9, 140-46, 157; as sacrifice, 6, 11-12, 97, 119, 136; as real presence, 5-7, 10-12, 14-16, 33-4, 91, 94-5

Fasting, 37, 133

Federal Council of Churches, 55-6, 58, 59, 70, 73, 74; *see* National Council of Churches

Fiske, G. W., 56, 58, 62, 64

Gospel procession, 118, 142-3

Gothic revival, 29, 45, 49

Gregorian chant, 25-6, 30, 35, 84

Guardini, R., 29, 32, 34

Guéranger, P., 24-6, 29

Hebert, A. G., 48, 113-14

Heiler, F., 42, 84

Holy Orders, *see* Ministry

Holy Spirit, 13-15, 16, 154-5

Hymns, 62, 68-9, 142

Icons, 10

International Liturgical Conferences and Weeks, 31, 37-8

Invocation, *see Epiclesis*
Iona Community, 44, 76

Ladd. W. P., 4, 48
Lietzmann, H., 30, 42
Liturgiology, 10, 27-9, 32, 43-4
　47, 48-9, 84-5, 86
Loehe, W., 41, 83
Lutheran Liturgical Association,
　43, 86, 90
Lutherans, 28, 30, 40-43, 63, 70,
　73, 74, 78, 82-97, 139

Maria Laach, 4, 10, 26, 32, 34,
　37-8, 39
Mariolatry, 96
Maxwell, W. D., 43, 44, 57, 76
Mercersburg Movement, 44
Methodists, 41, 61, 67, 71, 74,
　77-8, 79
Michonneau, Abbé, 40, 104
Military chapels, 73-4
Ministry, 91, 93, 95-6, 111-12
Morning Prayer, 133-4, 137-8
Mystery theology, 4-7, 8, 10-13,
　26, 33-4, 123

National Council of Churches, 57,
　70, 80

Offertory procession, 118, 143-4
Orate Fratres, see *Worship*
Orchard, W. E., 50, 59
Otto, R., 6-7, 16, 33, 41-2

Parish council, 125-30
Pietism, 41, 103
Pius X, 24, 25, 30
Pius XII, 24, 36-7, 39

Preaching, 81, 87, 112, 142
Presbyterians, *see* Reformed
　Churches

Reformation, 10, 13, 28, 40-41,
　47, 61, 82-3, 90, 92
Reformed Churches, 40, 43-5, 52,
　66-7, 76-7
Roman Catholicism, 3, 4-7, 11-12,
　16-17, 21-40, 42, 45, 46, 48, 50,
　63, 64, 70, 73, 74, 88-9, 94, 104,
　112, 119
Romanticism, 24, 27, 45

St. John's Abbey, 3, 31, 35
St. Luke, Order of, 77-8
Scotland, Church of, 43-4, 76
Solesmes, Abbey of, 24, 25-6
South India, Church of, 52, 107-8,
　110
Sperry, W. L., 50, 55, 56, 102
Symbolical Books, 87, 91, 92, 93-4,
　95, 96, 97

Taizé Community, 45, 77
Thirkield, W. P., 56, 58, 63
Transubstantiation, 6-7, 10-12, 13,
　94-5

Una Sancta, 43, 57, 86, 88

Vonier, A., 5, 14

Women, ministry of, 115-18
Words of Institution, 9-10, 11,
　90-91, 140
Worship, 35, 57